Be a person who loves and is loved.
You, too, can experience
the amazing power of forgiveness
— the secret to an open heart.

THE KEY TO AN
Open Heart

THE KEY TO AN

Open Heart

KAREN BURTON MAINS

DAVID C. COOK PUBLISHING CO.
ELGIN, ILLINOIS

Grateful acknowledgement is made to the following publishers for permission to reprint copyrighted material:

"At a Window" from CHICAGO POEMS by Carl Sandburg, copyright 1916 by Holt, Rinehart and Winston, Inc.; copyright 1944 by Carl Sandburg. Reprinted by permission of Harcourt Brace Jovanovich, Inc.

"Forgiveness, Another Word for Love" reprinted from SIDEWALK PSALMS © 1979 by Good News Publishers, Westchester, IL 60153. Used by permission.

"Grant Me the Kind of Love" reprinted from I NEED A MIRACLE TODAY, LORD by Wilma Burton. Copyright 1976. Moody Press, Moody Bible Institute of Chicago. Used by permission.

"The Old Stone House" reprinted from THE COMPLETE POEMS © 1969. Literary trustees of Walter de la Mare and the Society of authors as their representatives. Used by permission.

"The Revolutionary" reprinted from LISTEN TO THE GREEN © 1971 by Luci Shaw, Harold Shaw Publishers, Wheaton, IL 60187. Used by permission.

THE SINGER by Calvin Miller © 1975 by Inter Varsity Christian Fellowship. Used by permission of Inter Varsity Press.

Published by David C. Cook Publishing Co., Elgin, IL 60120
Printed in the United States of America
Library of Congress Catalog Number: 79-51746
ISBN 0-89191-184-7 (hardcover)
ISBN 0-89191-947-3 (paperback)

ISBN 1-55513-198-0 (paperback with additional Bible Study)

To my grandmother, Nellie Ruth Branham,
who is my prototype
of the housekeeper in our souls

Acknowledgments

I am grateful for the pioneering work of Agnes Sanford, on which much of the structure of this book is based.

And I wish to thank Jim Hilt, psychological counselor, for inspection of this book; he tested the shingles to see if they were straight and made sure that the doors opened and closed with ease.

Contents

Contents

Nothing on the grey roof, nothing on the brown,
Only a little greening where the rain drips down;
Nobody at the window, nobody at the door,
Only a little hollow which a foot once wore;
But still I tread on tiptoe, still tiptoe on I go,
Past nettles, porch, and weedy well, for oh, I know
A friendless face is peering, and a clear still eye
Peeps closely through the casement as my step goes by.

"THE OLD STONE HOUSE"
Walter de la Mare

ONE

Cramped Spaces, Narrow Hallways, Locked Doors

In the middle of our town sits an old house that still bears hints of grandness, despite the fact that it has been abandoned for as long as I can remember. I was raised in this locale, married here, and eventually moved with my husband to explore life in a nearby brawling city. Now we are dwelling once more, after a thirteen-year odyssey, at home. The old house has never been occupied through any of that passing time.

Once its lawns were wide, but through the years the flower gardens and planting beds have been devoured in bite-sized chunks by hungry home builders. The woefully small yard that now remains is obviously disproportionate to the tall house quietly moldering beneath its flaking paint.

"There's the ghost house again!" one of our little ones cries whenever we drive past the structure. His sense of romance demands this sort of appellation. But to me, an adult, it is the "fine old house" because I can see in it the vestiges of better years.

Those wide porches once hosted visitors who sat in rocking chairs sipping lemonade on hot summer afternoons. The porches are empty now. That imposing front door once banged in alternate rhythms, keeping time to the coming and going of many children. It is now locked—I have never seen it open.

The lawn is trimmed. Some hired agent keeps it under control, but there is no love in it. The grass creeps dully up to the foundations. No geraniums bob in summer rains, no herbs border kitchen gardens, no purple plums soften the harsh angularity of this frame structure.

No, the windows stare vacantly at their adjoining neighbors. They peer, hollow eyed. No dimity curtains float with the breeze. No plants are moved from place to place to catch the light. No people pass from room to room. No fires burn. No children practice laryngitic clarinets or squealing violins in the music room.

Oh, if only someone would give it a fresh coat of paint, I think to myself, building nests in somebody else's tree. *A few shutters here, a bright color on the door, a brick walk, and bushes to hide the cement slip.* It would take so little to make the old place elegant again.

I never pass that street without thinking what fun it would be to see that old house in the middle of our town renovated. If someone would only buy it and love it and live in it and throw those windows open wide! But no one buys (perhaps it is not for sale; I have never seen a sign), and no one paints. No one creaks open the windows and lets the fresh Midwestern prairie wind scent the rooms with the smells of grain and grass. The neglect

14

of such a fine old house seems almost obscene.

Occasionally I think of it as a silent memorial to some past disaster: perhaps a murder within its walls. Or perhaps it is the legacy of a proud family, now disinherited, which can no longer afford its upkeep. One thing is sure: this place was meant for living. For some unknown reason, its purpose has been denied.

I am familiar with the wear and tear of living. We are continually taking three steps backward for every five forward with our houseful of children. Grimy fingerprints regularly stencil our fresh coats of wall paint. I clearly remember the seven windows broken over the period of a year by one boy, practicing his baseball arm.

Yet the wear and tear from disuse is as damaging, I think, as that havocked on material things by lively families. The damage of neglect, of windows jamming on their pulleys, of doors rusting on their hinges, of rooms and hallways settling under the accumulating years of dust and darkness—all these are as extensive and disheartening as wear caused by the rough and tumble of rowdy, normal living.

Often I am asked, "Why is it that there are certain types of people it is impossible for me to love?" The companion question is similar: "Why is it so difficult to love one another in the Body of Christ?"

At first, I used to think this type of approach was simply rationalization, lame excuses for not bringing one's heart into line with loving. I have since discovered that these people were right. There are some humans I can't love.

Sometimes even a child under my own roof is impossible. Perhaps an in-law or a parent brings me nothing but pain. That cantankerous neighbor churns my stomach with wooden paddles of complaints. For some, a husband is unfaithful, a friend turns his back, a wife's

15

venom bites like an adder does.

There are people as well in the Body of Christ that I can't love. A pastor is cold and unfeeling. The contentious group has split over a doctrinal issue, dividing the congregation and bringing down upon our heads the scorn of the town. A youth pastor has been fired—some think it was unfair, others insist it was justified. An elder has been unrighteous. A Christian brother has betrayed my confidence.

The world is not large enough, I suppose, to hold the reasons for not loving.

Yet there are also numerous examples of "impossible" love—love for one's captor, love for the impoverished—which are supernatural, far beyond that which most of us are personally capable. Still, if others can do it, why can't we? Why are we so incapacitated when it comes to this matter of loving?

Very simply, the reason is that our hearts have become boarded. They are as barricaded and unused as the fine old house standing empty and locked in the middle of my town.

The household of God, that spiritual dwelling place for the joint heirs in Christ, has also ceased functioning as intended. It is no longer a hospice, a shelter, a sanctuary. It is no longer a way station for healing. It has become a fortification, not for fighting the battles waging outside its walls, but for stockading against others who live within.

Christ frequently used the household as an illustration of spiritual truth. Luke 11:24-26 reads, "When the unclean spirit has gone out of a man, he passes through waterless places seeking rest; and finding none he says, 'I will return to my house from which I came.' And when he comes he finds it swept and put in order. Then he goes and brings seven other spirits more evil than himself, and they enter and dwell there; and the last state of that man becomes worse than the first."

Luke 6: 47, 48 reveals the familiar parable of the house on the rock: "Every one who comes to me and hears my words and does them, I will show you what he is like: he is like a man building a house, who dug deep, and laid the foundation upon rock; and when a flood arose, the stream broke against that house, and could not shake it, because it had been well built."

The accusations of the Pharisees who insisted that Christ cast out demons by the power of the prince of demons was answered with, "Every kingdom divided against itself is laid waste, and a divided household falls."

It is an allegory that I love. For some reason, I think of the heart as a household, one with many rooms. I agree with Oliver Wendell Holmes when he wrote "Build thee more stately mansions, O my soul." There is a mansion in our souls for which we need to take intimate responsibility. There is a spiritual household of God, a corporate mystical dwelling, that is standing in disuse and neglect.

I am amazed at how often I encounter this symbol of the house in my dreams. As much as I love the out-of-doors, these dramas of the subconscious rarely take place there. I am most likely to find myself in a house with many rooms, many windows, many doors.

I remember one dream that gave me pause. When we were pastoring in the inner city of Chicago, I dreamed that I was in a large apartment at the top of a tall sky-scraper. It was my home. A strong and gentle wind blew through the open windows, swaying the building, yet I was not afraid. From time to time different members of our congregation entered the front door, until the apart-ment was quite full. As people arrived, I gave each one a gift. I had no idea what was in any package, but I re-

17

member feeling that every one was precious and that I was extremely privileged to be the bearer of these items.

The strangest thing occurred as I gave away my gifts. The more I gave, the more rooms I discovered in my apartment! Here was an eating nook off the kitchen. How remarkable! I'd had no idea it was there. There was a lovely glassed-in porch overlooking the lake view—and an extra bedroom.

I am convinced this is the way it is with the habitation of our hearts. The more we love, the more room there is to love. I believe that when the Creator built into our beings that quality which enables us to love, he created it with an infinite capacity to embrace. We were intended to be loving creatures. He wanted us to have open hearts—nonprejudiced, nonpreferential, nondiscriminatory hearts.

But his original design was turned topsy-turvy. Sin entered the creation, entered the creature. We as humans are simply incapable of dealing with sin, either our own or that of others against us. The habitation of the heart no longer rambles over open spaces—a wide veranda here, a turret spiraling there, a new wing sprawling to the side. Its territory has become sharply defined.

We are consequently the possessors of mean rooms—damp basements, narrow hallways, cramped spaces. Something unnatural has occurred. This place God created to be open to the fresh wind of his Spirit, the dwelling he desires to occupy in order that it may be habitable to others, has become boarded. The windows are shuttered, the blinds drawn. Dust is accumulating. The doors have been padlocked. No daylight shines in. Our hearts are no longer lovable places.

Often we ourselves are responsible for this "fine old house" standing neglected in the middle of our souls. We have wielded the hammer. Our own hands have pounded nails against the wood. We have sinned.

Often someone else has bolted the lock. Through no consent of our own, another's careless hands have posted a sign which reads, NO TRESPASSING! VIOLATORS WILL BE PROSECUTED! Someone has sinned against us.

The results of our own sins and those of others are the same. Our souls are hidden in boarded dwellings; our hearts captured in uninhabitable houses. People pass us by and wish, "Oh, if only she could be given a fresh coat of paint! If only someone would unlock that door and make this a lived-in place once again!"

Unfortunately, the effect of boarded hearts within the church, the family of God, is cumulative. It is the withholding of love from one another, the coming together of these handicapped hearts, that causes fortification in our souls. We face each other from defensive positions, "peeping closely from the casements."

So I have finally learned that there are people it is impossible for me to love. There are members in the very family of Christ toward whom my heart remains shut. The doors to my soul have become locked. Entry is forbidden.

Fortunately, our Creator in his great love has crafted a key that unlocks our fortified towers. It is a master key that opens all rooms, turns all rusty tumblers. Without it, we can only occupy the territory of the heart by breaking and entering.

It is only with this key that the front door, creaking and groaning on its ancient hinges, can be pushed open for those who long for an invitation to come in. It is only after the door has been pushed open to each house, to each room, that we can walk about, raising blinds in order to bask in the bright sunlight, to breathe the fresh wind of the Spirit. It is only after this key has been turned that we can begin to sweep away the accumulated filth.

The key that opens the door to the locked rooms of our hearts is forgiveness. It is only when we have experienced forgiveness (and I cannot emphasize strongly enough that I am not talking about the simple nodding of one's head to a preacher's words; I mean being *overwhelmed* by the reality of forgiveness, being able to touch, taste, and smell its results) *that* we find the locks are sprung, the doors flung open, the windows tossed high, the rooms inhabited, and fires lighted on the hearths.

It is then we discover that our hearts are finally free to love. They have become what the Creator intended them to be, places with immense capacity to embrace. We may even hear ourselves saying with surprise, "Do you know, *there isn't anyone I can't love!*" Then we will discover that God has done his work in us.

LIFE RESPONSE

I once was asked to list the names of all the people I didn't love. At first I loudly protested, "Why there isn't anyone I don't love!" I even maintained (foolishly) that I had an exceptional ability to love.

My Questioner persisted, and because he is One who will not be turned lightly aside, I began the work of naming. There were twenty-seven names!

If that same Inquisitor were to ask you the identical question, how long would your list be?

Take a few moments in private. Write down the names of those in your family, your church, or your world that you don't love. Then pray this prayer: O Lord, heavenly Father, teach me the meaning of loving. Help me to learn to unlock the doors to my closed heart.

One need not be a Chamber—to be Haunted—
One need not be a House—
The Brain has Corridors—surpassing
Material Place—

Far safer, of a Midnight Meeting
External Ghost
Than its interior Confronting—
That Cooler Host.

Far safer, through an Abbey gallop,
The stones a'chase—
Than Unarmed, one's a'self encounter—
In lonesome Place—

Ourself behind ourself, concealed—
Should startle most—
Assassin hid in our Apartment
Be Horror's least.

The Body—borrows a Revolver—
He bolts the Door—
O'erlooking a superior spectre—
Or More—

Emily Dickinson

TWO
Haunted Corridors

Normally, I abhor oatmeal. Ever since my father forced me to swallow a spoonful as I dawdled over breakfast when I was four or five, the thought of that food has been nauseating to me. I did, on that long-ago day, what any child would do when faced with an overzealous parent: I vomited it back, all over daddy. Since then I haven't been able to stand the sight, smell, or taste of the stuff.

On one summer's day, though, while I was attending a conference on psychological healing, I discovered that something unusual had happened to me. After years of abhorrence, I suddenly found I could eat oatmeal!

I had attended this week-long retreat for the express purpose of finding spiritual methods that could help the psychologically and emotionally distressed individuals in our congregation. My husband was pastoring an inner-city church in the heart of Chicago. We had discovered that the peculiar nature of our body—nontraditional in structure and worship; emphatic in its insistence that God's love is for the individual no matter how broken or estranged—attracted many people who had been damaged in their past.

Homosexuals came seeking hope and change. We listened as they revealed to us the despair of their struggles, the awkward parenting in the past that had left them vulnerable to this condition.

Feminists, many of them angry women, formed a study and pressure group. Educated and highly intelligent, they were discovering the limitations imposed upon their sex in job markets (despite their costly diplomas) and in the church (regardless of their burgeoning intellects). We listened to their rage and attempted to assuage it.

Blacks came to the church. The underprivileged edged timidly to our doors. We learned something of the sticky, entangled webs of societal prejudice and economic debilitation—the subtle inheritances of poverty. We learned firsthand how ephemeral is human trust, how transitory.

Rubbing backs with every psychiatric diagnosis possible, we pasted hopeless bandaids on massive wounds of the psyche. One disturbed young man started a worship service by standing in the back of the hall and shouting out a string of obscenities. Then he ran from our auditorium. It was rather an amazing "call to worship!"

From the front, David asked the congregation to bow their heads in prayer. "We are not going to allow this to disrupt our purpose for this morning," he explained quietly. "We have come to adore. Our hearts will go

24

about the business of worship. But right now, before we begin, I want us to think about this young man. He needs our love. Listen now to the voice of the Spirit. There will be some of you that He is telling to give away that love." In the silence, several rose and went out, while the rest of us proceeded with the morning service.

Our hearts were willing enough. They simply weren't wide or deep enough to embrace. We failed to reach the pits into which so many had descended.

There were times when we wondered if there were any who were whole among us! David began referring to our congregation as "David's band," quoting from 1 Samuel 22:2, "And every one who was in distress, and every one who was in debt, and every one who was discontented, gathered to him; and he became captain over them."

After a while, we came to the end of our human resources. We had listened to the same tales of woe over and over again, witnessed the same promises to do better, the same false starts. There must be something more, we concluded. There must be something beyond our paltry, elastic solutions for strained emotions, our unhealing potions for soul wounds. There must be a spiritual poultice for the sores we watched festering in so many spirits. There must be a power of God available to touch and heal these deep illnesses of the psyche.

Was God who he said he was, or not? Was he able? Was he all powerful? Did he intervene in our human affairs? The answers were basic to the future of my faith.

Desperate to discover some solutions for that band God had brought under our care, I attended a conference on inner healing. I went to help others and unexpectedly found help for myself.

Having received a scholarship from a friend of my brother, I found myself at a campgrounds of a United Methodist church, rooming with three Catholic nuns.

The conference was led by a Southern Baptist minister, a United Methodist minister, and an Episcopalian layperson. Here I was a child of the fundamentalists, whose father had been on the faculty of Moody Bible Institute for three decades! The inner city will do strange things to people.

I loved the marvelous prebreakfast worship times. The singing was spontaneous and full hearted, the Scripture sweet. To begin each day with formal matins (morning prayer) has always been my secret longing.

The fellowship of all this diversity was, to say the least, unique. My bunkmates and I spent many a hilarious hour discovering common negative holdovers from our different church backgrounds. The modes were dissimilar; the legalism was the same. It was a time of rich feeding for me, turning my eyes to the fact that Christ's Body is alive and well in the most surprising places.

In one of our teaching sessions we were asked to review the stages of our past and attempt to discover any remnant memories that might still cause us pain. Apart from a certain incident with my father and the oatmeal, my childhood memories were happy and warm. However, I did recognize one portion of my life that held residual pain.

I was raised in Wheaton, Illinois, which is a center for countless evangelical ministries. My growing up was interwined with many of these organizations, including mission societies, churches, the college, and national youth headquarters. My mother had worked in a secretarial capacity for various groups; our social life had moved within this framework; and my husband's early ministries were scattered among these organizations.

As I looked into the past I realized I had some painful memories about the town of Wheaton! I could hardly return there, a forty-five-minute drive from the city, without evoking some negative emotions. I had stated frankly that I never wanted to live there again. In fact, the less I had to do with the place, the better.

Emotions are often like the mixed strands of tumbled yarns. We need to trace one hue in order to get back to the original skein. Unwinding these sentiments, I discovered that a lot of my negative feelings were associated with some of the Christian leaders with whom we had worked in that town. Some had had feet of clay. Some had been less than what we hoped they would be. There was personal disappointment over these elders' failures—but there was something more.

Suddenly, I came in touch with the source of my confused strands—with the original ball. Most of the men with whom we had worked had, in one way or another, closed their hearts to my husband. Looking back, I couldn't find one who had discipled him. There was no older man who had reached out to a younger man coming up in the ministry. No one had given him loving discipline when he needed it. No one had even given him words of encouragement. The president of one organization went so far as to tell David that he might as well face it, he'd never be a preacher. (David may have been bad, but he wassn't that bad! Besides, he was only twenty-six.)

The only encouragement I could remember was casual. Once someone grabbed my husband's arm in the aisle of Moody Memorial Church, after we had moved from Wheaton and were serving in an associate pastor capacity. He said, "Keep with it, David. We need young men like you in the ministry." That was all, but *I* had noted it well.

After close scrutiny, I discovered that I was suffering from the withholding of love. There had been no overt act against me that was causing me pain. It was the result of unintentional neglect, pure and simple. What's more, it wasn't even my own pain. It was David's, but he hadn't picked it up—I had!

I attended the workshop that afternoon loaded with new understanding. As we began to examine each section of our life, and to pray about them all, we were asked to forgive those people who had been the source of our emotional distress. I realized I had never forgiven those men who had withheld their love from my husband! Perhaps they had been weary in ministry, perhaps they had been in pain, perhaps they had been suffering from the effects of *others* not loving *them*. I needed to forgive them; they deserved to be forgiven.

After the working hour together, I hurried down to the beachfront, forgoing dinner. There was some soul feeding I needed to undergo first. Nestling into the sun-warmed hollow of an old gray rock that sat beside the gentle ebbings of Lake Michigan, I took my prayer notebook and began the work of forgiveness—the first I can remember consciously undertaking.

"I forgive . . ." I scrawled, then wrote each name, specifically listing the action (or mostly lack of action) that had caused me pain. "I forgive _____ for telling David he would never be a preacher. I forgive his lack of wisdom in giving this unencouraging and hopeless evaluation to an eager young man. I forgive . . ."

The list went on and on. When I had filled a page and a half, suddenly the dams within me began to break. Something supernatural touched my internal being, and I began to weep and weep. My emotional pain was as real as though those acts of neglect had been committed that week, as though those unintentional rejections had occurred yesterday. What's more, I understood that I was suffering from the cumulative effects of the withholding of love, and that my pain incurred over the process of

28

years, was being dealt with in the space of an hour or so.

I don't know how long the emotional catharsis continued—dinner was long over by the time I was done. I had missed a meal, and I went to bed with an empty stomach—but my soul was full and satisfied.

Needless to say, I rose the next morning quite hungry. Hurrying to the dining hall, I happened to sit by one of the leaders of the retreat. I was sharing with him what I thought God had been doing in my life when the breakfast menu was served. I could smell it coming. We were having oatmeal that morning.

"Well," I quipped facetiously, "I'll know I've been healed if I can eat *that!*"

Much to my surprise, I ate the whole bowl! Up to that point I couldn't even prepare cooked cereal for my children without the odor of it turning my stomach, and now I had just polished off a full portion without one tiny wave of nausea.

How often God bends himself to accommodate our tiny armspans of faith. The fact that I can, to this day, eat a bowl of oatmeal, is a physical reminder of a supernatural work in me. The liturgical churches call this an act of his "grace," a tangible symbol to remember the invisible work of God's love in my soul.

Something amazing happened to me when I returned to our congregation. I discovered that because of my deliberate act of forgiveness toward those in my past who had withheld their love, I was now free to love those same types of people who populated my present! Some door on the inside of me had been opened. It was no longer closed to the people who now gave me pain.

The heart is an amazing thing. It is at once complicated and simple. My reaction to the withholding of love in the past was keeping me from giving love to those who were withholding love from us in the present.

Our congregation was composed of the generation of the sixties, and our average age was twenty-eight. Our peers were disrupting campuses, holding sit-ins, and marching in protests. It was an analytical, angry, and activist age. In many ways we were the ecclesiastical children of our decade.

It was only natural, I suppose, that our church would mirror the times. Our protests were quieter, less violent, but as real. Antiauthoritarian, critical of leadership, we had one fatal flaw: a complete misunderstanding of the role of authority. Our difficulty stemmed from more than outright rebellion. My generation, and particularly that generation following mine, seemed to have no positive models of leadership.

One of the difficult problems with which every pastor must cope is that of psychological transference, the application of misplaced emotional reactions onto the authority figure—himself. In our congregation—with their intense need to intellectualize every decision, to resist any firm leadership, to insist that each individual be involved in pursuing any new directions—it was a problem magnified multiple times. David became a focus for criticism, and we found that, invariably, the people who had the greatest difficulty with him were victims of unhappy relationships with authority (father) figures in their past.

Slam! The doors banged shut within me, and I kept them shut. I simply could not love the critical people of our congregation. I could barely be civil. The tragedy of this is, of course, the classic unbroken cycle of sin—I cannot love them because they cannot love me because I cannot love them. . . . Frequently the people from whom we withhold our love are most in need of it, and this makes our human dilemmas even sadder.

Talk about transference! The way I picked up my husband's griefs was incredible. (I have since discovered that many of us carry a loved one's pains.) And each new grievance turned the screws on my heart's padlocks a little tighter.

Forgiveness was the key. I forgave those in my past who had caused me pain. When I forgave those in my yesterday, the doors were opened to love people critical of my husband's ministry today. Simple, really—and also terribly complex. Another puzzling result is that the negative feelings toward my hometown dissolved! I discovered that I could "go home."

At any rate, at the end of the conference, I asked the leaders to send me away with their prayers that I might be filled with God's love. I went back to discover that something supernatural had indeed occurred. There wasn't anyone I couldn't *learn* to love. Unarmed, I had encountered myself in a lonesome place. The "superior spectre" had been met. My heart was no longer a haunted place. I was free to throw the front door wide open to all who might be seeking entry.

LIFE RESPONSE

A young woman who came to me was suffering from a chronic case of shyness that was particularly painful to her in group situations. Looking into her past, we discovered a third-grade teacher who had continually humiliated her in front of her classmates. My friend forgave that long-ago teacher. She is now a gregarious socializer! The past no longer haunts her present.

Check the corridors of your past, all the life stages. Are any of those passages haunted? Use the following check sheet for a memory review. If there are any painful residual memories, jot down the circumstances, the people, or the places that caused you pain. Ask the Holy Spirit to be a companion as you undertake the journey back.

Early childhood—infancy to the start of school.
Grade school years—through the sixth grade.
Junior and high school years—the teen years.
Early adulthood—include college, trade school, early marriage, starting a profession.
The twenties
The thirties
The forties
The fifties
The sixties
The seventies
The eighties

The Soul selects her own Society—
Then—shuts the Door—
To her divine Majority—
Present no more—

Unmoved—she notes the Chariots—pausing—
At her low Gate—
Unmoved—an Emperor be kneeling
Upon her Mat—

Emily Dickinson

THREE
Interior Territory

Traveling home from Phoenix, Arizona, recently, I discovered I had left my satchel with all my carefully organized papers headed "Things-to-do," my research reading, even my Bible, in the backseat of the car of the lovely woman who had rushed me to the airport.

Chagrined, I thought about my subtle inward pride. How smug I had felt (wearing my new high heels and my tailored suit) flying out from Chicago. I remembered how self-satisfied I had been over the most recent printer's galleys I had efficiently edited on the plane, how secretly elated I had been that my journey was not strictly pleasure. *I* was one of the 20 percent of women who regularly traveled on "business."

And now all my work was in a car, bobbing over the Arizona desert, and a three- and a-half-hour, no-turning-back flight stretched before me. My latent inefficiency had brought me to grief again. I sighed. I knew why the Lord loved me; it was because I provided him with countless opportunities to chuckle.

"Thank you, Lord," I prayed, slightly chastened. "Thank you for this latest gaffe in a lifetime of gaffes. Thank you that it keeps me from being too pleased with myself. How do *you* intend for me to redeem this time?"

I prayed a little, but my mind was too restless for the work of intercession—my "business" had exhausted me. My seatmate seemed determined to sleep through the entire flight—no chance for conversation there. I exchanged seats with the woman behind me because I felt her plaster-casted leg would be more comfortable in my first-row, roomier chair. I held a young mother's infant to give her arms a rest, was honey-sweet to the stewards and stewardesses—but nothing. There were obviously no evangelistic trails to blaze on this crowded jet winging its way toward Chicago.

Resigned, I settled back and snatched the airways magazine from the seat pocket in front of me. One article entitled "Brainstorming" had an intriguing opening:

"Inside our heads," wrote author Richard Wokkomir, "it's pure Alice in Wonderland. And the neuro-explorers now adventuring down the brain's rabbit holes are discovering all sorts of magic mushrooms: Current brain research may lead to cures for disorders ranging from diabetes and schizophrenia to the chronic inability to remember one's Social Security number.

"They're also bumping into electro-chemical Cheshire cats. Indeed, we're turning out to be more enchanted and complicated creatures than we ever knew."

Upon returning home, I did some more research about

the brain. I discovered that the human mind is a wonder of all God's marvelous creations! Scientists once compared the brain to a loom . . . then to a telephone system . . . then to a computer. Now they know that such technological comparisons are woefully primitive. For example, an advanced computer may have more than seventy-seven-hundred printed circuits, requiring seventy miles of wiring to hook up its two million "memory cells." But this is only a feeble illustration of the complexity of the human brain with its billions of interconnected nerve blocks.

Networks of these cells run throughout the body, intertwining every tissue with the 10 billion nerve cells of the governing city, the brain. Electrical impulses rush along these expressways at speeds ranging from two- to two-hundred miles an hour, leaping across narrow bridges between cells, commandeering intelligence to and from the brain.

Research into this small, four-pound organ has become a complicated science. It is concerned with more than the anatomical examination of the gray matter within our skulls: the simple locating of the brainstem, the cerebellum, the cerebral hemispheres. It probes the intertwined sciences of psychology, philosophy, behaviorology, linguistic physiology, mental normality and abnormality, hypnosis, drugs and thought control, ad infinitum, and leads us to conclude with the National Science Foundation spokesman that the brain is "the most complex and functionally dense mass of matter known in the universe."

A well-worn illustration of the mind compares it to an iceberg: the tip is the conscious mind and the submerged part is the subconscious. God has entrusted us with responsibility for the conscious mind. This is the will of man, that thinking arena God seeks to persuade but refuses to transgress in any way.

The subconscious is the source of our feelings and emotions. I believe that this vast hidden territory, brooding beneath the waters of consciousness, is designed to respond to the spiritual. This mysterious, subterranean zone is too unplotted for many successful human journeys, but it is well tracked by the Spirit. He understands it implicitly. Our human responsibility for the subconscious must include an expectancy that God is able and will intervene in this confusing terrain by his supernatural touch.

Whether modern man recognizes it or not, he is dependent upon supernatural revelation to understand his own subconscious. This is the area of the mind that refuses to be test-tubed, synthesized, or examined under the microscope. Granted, more is known about it now than in any generation. But it still evades the formulation of concrete theory, laughing at the systematic diagrams that men insist on devising.

Yet we need to come to terms with the subconscious, because the conscious mind is continually influenced by it. As Eugene O'Neill says in his drama, *A Moon for the Misbegotten*, "There is no present or future—only the past, happening over and over again—now."

For the subconscious, in addition to being the source of our feelings and emotions, may also be a strange reservoir for all our memories. Experiments of the Canadian surgeon Dr. Wilder Penfield revealed that when areas of the brains of epileptic patients were stimulated by electrical currents, they would suddenly recall long-forgotten episodes out of their distant pasts with intense vividness. They would continue to recall more about each memory as long as the probes remained in the same place.

One of the possible conclusions to be drawn from this

is that all the memories, all the experiences of our lives, are stored in a certain record room of the brain, which is inexplicably linked to the subconscious.

We know that when certain areas of the brain are destroyed, the brain-damaged individual may have no memory. He lives in a state of suspended timelessness. This present moment is the only real moment that exists for him. He is an example of extreme existentialism. But just how this relates to the subconscious is unknown. All we do know is that time *doesn't* heal all wounds. Sometimes past pain can be evoked as freshly as if it had just occurred. We are all potentially bondslaves to our yesterdays.

The subconscious is continually in distress because of our one great human dilemma: sin. We were not intended to be carriers of these distresses. Our fragile souls were not meant to be depositories for such disease. Our natural condition is innocence. Instinctively, we long for Eden. And this longing is the source of our ancient fascination with Utopias, our endless attempts to create Camelots that are all doomed to failure, sentenced by our own human flaws.

The discomfort of sin may come in one of two ways. It may be our own sin against which our subconscious struggles. All of us carry about unreconciled guilt due to shameful or ugly or petty things we have done. This is true moral guilt. We have broken a moral code, an absolute law that exists. In fact, C.S. Lewis maintains that the existence of an absolute moral code can be concluded from the fact that we do feel guilt. Guilt is God's unbearable gift to us in order that we might turn to righteous living.

The subconscious may also be struggling with the effects of others' sins against us. These sins may be real or imagined. They may be intentional acts against us, attempts on the part of others to give us pain, to damage us; or they may be acts that were not consciously intended, blows the offender never realized he dealt. It is amazing how seldom humans know that they have hurt one another.

It is my personal belief that we suffer more frequently from the inadvertent acts than from the deliberate ones. Most people do not know they have hurt us. At any rate, real or imagined, intended or inadvertent, the results are the same: pain. What's more, we are tethered by an incapability to deal effectively with the effects of sin.

Our human inability to cope with sin, either our own or that of others against us, is the crux of our incredible alienation from our own selves and from one another. The subconscious suffers from our own guilt, the result of our own sin. It quails in the face of another's deliberate or ignorant act against us and the subsequent grief.

One of the techniques for bearing pain that resides in the conscious mind is to bury it in the deep reservoir of the subconscious. But even the psychological devices we have evolved to help us coexist peacefully with the pain of our past are eventually counterproductive.

I like to think of the subconscious as a huge house. It rambles in the soul with many rooms and porticos still undiscovered. The conscious mind takes an unbearable thing, something that will inhibit normal daily functioning, and shoves it into one of the rooms of the subconscious. It slams the door and thinks, "There! That takes care of *that!*"

Now the household of the soul is inhabited by what Agnes Sanford calls, "a tidy housekeeper." It is her role to keep the rooms of the subconscious in order. She is on assignment from the Creator. On one of her cleansing forays, she discovers the closed room, opens the door, and tosses that unseemly article back up to the conscious mind and shouts, "Here, you get rid of *this!*" The subconscious is demanding innocence—a return to sinlessness.

Our conscious mind is suddenly aware of something forgotten. We experience a flash of memory. We recall the unpleasant past. There is a haunting remembrance. A word spoken by someone whispers of buried pain.

Because we are human, alienated from the Creator who understands the territory of the subconscious, we are helpless before the dilemma of sin. We do not know how to handle our painful memory, so we renew our efforts. We repeat the first burial with increased vigor. We shove that sudden rush of memory into another room in the household of our soul. We bolt the windows, pull the shades, lock the door, padlock it, nail a sign on it that reads, DO NOT DISTURB!—and think we have healed ourselves. We deceive ourselves with forgetfulness.

The result of all this is eventually tragic. After years of responding to sin in this fashion, we begin to experience its cumulative effect. Many rooms within the house of the subconscious have become boarded and shut. If the shades are drawn in a room, the sun cannot shine in and we cannot see out. If many rooms remain this way, the house becomes a dark and unlighted place. If the kitchen pantry is stocked with venom and the living room is unused, the house is not functioning as it was intended. It is an uncomfortable place for those who live there and an unwelcome place to others who seek to enter.

Jesus summarized the Old Testament Law in one terse directive. "Teacher, which is the great commandment in the law?" queried a lawyer. The reply was, "You shall love the Lord your God with all your heart, and with all your soul, and with all your mind. This is the great and first commandment. And a second is like it, You shall love your neighbor as yourself. On these two commandments depend all the law and the prophets" (Matt. 22:36-40).

The tragedy of boarded hearts, barricaded souls, padlocks on the subconscious is that God's love is blocked as it seeks to fill us. We are incapable of receiving him; we are debilitated in responding to him as Christ directed, *with all our heart*. "Behold, I stand at the door and knock" read the words of Christ from Revelation. "If any one hears my voice and opens the door, I will come in to him and eat with him, and he with me" (3:20). It is our sins that have double-bolted the door, and it is our fearful sinfulness that keeps us from removing the chain.

Our dilemma is compounded—now we begin to enact the cycle of human tragedy. We withhold love from our fellow humans. Intentionally or unintentionally, we give them grief. We are helpless to love our neighbor as ourself.

A wise woman tried to teach me that it is a sin to withhold love from any person. I have since become convinced that she is right. Whenever I close the door to my heart, I am sinning. Whenever I draw the shade to my soul in order to shut out the passerby, I am transgressing. Whenever race or creed or nationality becomes an excuse for padlocking, I have erred. It *is* a sin to withhold love from any person.

Furthermore, pastoral counseling has convinced me that it is the withholding of love that is the source of most of our emotional and psychological damage. A friend no longer desires my company. An in-law refuses to be interested in my essential and unique self. A child rebels and no telephone, letter, or rumor brings any message of his whereabouts. Slam! Slam! go the doors. I am damaged because I have closed my heart. You are damaged because I have withheld love from you.

Thus we are trapped by our incredible barriers of human alienation. We have become boarded, abandoned dwellings, fine old houses in the middle of town, moldering beneath flaking paint. The immense capacity of the heart to embrace has become restrained.

Our hearts have, indeed, become stone.

LIFE RESPONSE

Any of the journeys that we take are risky. A car can collide in heavy traffic. An airplane might overshoot the runway. It is possible to become confused in new surroundings and lose our way.

How comforting it is to know that when we attempt to cross the unplotted territory of the subconscious, we can have a Guide who is familiar with the terrain. Compose a short prayer inviting the Holy Spirit to be by your side for the rest of this journey. Ask him to point out special sights you might overlook, to insure that you won't make any false turns (unless they are absolutely necessary), to guarantee that you won't become a traffic fatality.

Then anticipate the traveling ahead. Surprises are always in store with this remarkable tour guide! You may see scenery you never anticipated. You may meet delightful people or make engaging new acquaintances.

Keep in mind that the purpose of this journey is to find your way. A few mountains to climb, some stones in your shoes, or some aching muscles are well worth the treasure waiting at the end.

Build thee more stately mansions, O my soul,
 As the swift seasons roll!
 Leave thy low-vaulted past!
Let each new temple, nobler than the last,
Shut thee from heaven with a dome more vast,
 Till thou at length art free,
Leaving thine outgrown shell by life's unresting sea!

"THE CHAMBERED NAUTILUS"
Oliver Wendell Holmes

FOUR
The Tidy Housekeeper

My father had a favorite expression to describe his mother-in-law, my grandmother. He used to say, "Nellie is a whirlwind in reverse. Everywhere she goes, things fly *into* place!"

It is true. All my memories of childhood are filled with visions of gram—putting cleanliness into our home, making lovely garments for me from still-good, but discarded material. Windows shone brightly, it seemed, soon after she entered a room. Curtains hung starched, militarily straight, having shed their winter's dust for her. Sleeping quarters were immediately aired. The sheets lay folded on the beds, stiff with freshness—all this in one magic moment of my grandmother's turning around!

"How do you get the sheets so fresh?" I remember asking when I was newly married, hoping gram would reveal some secret formula. "A little bluing and some bleach," she replied. It was exactly what I used, but my sheets were still sheets. The ones she washed had that distinctive aura of an exclusive hotel.

Perhaps the secret ingredient that set gram's cleaning apart from that of the common folk was her passion for order. She has spent her lifetime in an endless vendetta against dirt. The energy she has always brought to this private crusade is incredible. How often I have wished that I had half my gram's physical vitality.

My grandmother is in her eighties now, but it has not been too long since I watched her leap from a radiator onto the floor after scrubbing windows. Spry and trim, she has always been conscious of her waistline. I can remember thinking after watching her acrobatic feats, *I hope I can hop around like that in my seventies!*

The tidy housekeeper who dwells within the rooms of our subconscious is very much like my gram. She is a persistent housewife, fussing over dirt. She is totally dedicated to keeping that internal dwelling clean. Consequently, she has developed some effective means of gaining the attention of the conscious mind during this housecleaning process.

Often the first medium through which she chooses to communicate is the symbolic language of our dreams. There are two extreme attitudes we can take toward these unusual and hard-to-decipher messages. We can totally ignore them or we can be consumed by them.

I prefer to follow a middle-of-the-road position. I approach dreams with a casual attention, an unimpassioned watchfulness expressed well by the words of the poet Rilke in his *Letters to a Young Poet:* "Be patient towards all that is unsolved in your heart and try to love the

48

questions themselves like locked rooms and like books that are written in a very foreign tongue."

The first modern day attempt to associate dreams with the unconscious came from Sigmund Freud in his book, *The Interpretation of Dreams*. Freud believed that dreams were symbolic expressions of the individual's underlying sexual drives and inner conflicts. He believed in universal symbols; that certain symbols always drew direct conclusions or meaning. Freud has been criticized for his concentration on sex drives, his emphasis on universal symbols, and his denial of individual influences in the nature of dreams.

For example, when a person dreams about money, a novice may conclude that this always means that the dreamer is ambitious. However, money may symbolize greed and selfishness to the dreamer because of his particular experience.

There are a few, perhaps simplistic handles that have helped to give me handgrasps on the role dreams play in regard to our subconscious. First, I have come to terms with the fact that portions of Scripture regard dreams as messages to man. Often, God himself is reported to be the source of these communications.

In the thirty-first chapter of Genesis (v. 11), we have a record of two back-to-back incidents in which God communicated via dreams. Jacob explained to his critical brothers-in-law, the sons of Laban, "Then the angel of God said to me in the dream, 'Jacob,' and I said, 'Here I am!' " A few verses on (v. 24), we are told, "But God came to Laban the Aramean in a dream by night, and said to him, 'Take heed that you say not a word to Jacob, either good or bad.' "

The story of Joseph is like a case study in dreams. There is the prophetic unfolding given to the teenager, which revealed his future position of dominion over his own family. The retelling of this message incited his older brother to hatred teetering on fratricide. The brothers eventually sold young Joseph to a passing caravan, after first plotting his murder. Yet, undoubtedly, these same dreams sustained Joseph during the later, lonely years of exile in Egypt. There are the dreams of the butler and the baker, those of the Pharaoh, and the subsequent, correct decoding of them all.

In Numbers, God chastises Aaron and Miriam for their criticism of Moses with these intriguing words: "Hear my words: If there is a prophet among you, I the Lord make myself known to him in a vision, I speak with him in a dream. Not so with my servant Moses; he is entrusted with all my house. With him I speak mouth to mouth, clearly, and not in dark speech; and he beholds the form of the Lord" (12:6, 7). Moses was obviously a departure from the norm.

At Gibeon the Lord appeared to Solomon in a dream by night, and the new monarch requested the desire of his heart, the gift of wisdom to govern. In the New Testament, the angel of the Lord made a similar appearance to Joseph as he was contemplating the pregnant condition of his fiancee and determining how to divorce her privately. "Joseph, son of David, do not fear to take Mary your wife, for that which is conceived in her is of the Holy Spirit. . . ." The wife of Pilate pleaded with her husband during the trial of the Christ, "Have nothing to do with that righteous man, for I have suffered much over him today in a dream."

The writers of Scripture affirmed the role of the dream as a message-bearer of the subconscious.

Unfortunately, western man with his rationalistic mind, including modern objective man in the church, must struggle to accept anything that deals with the subconscious. It is a large pill for him to swallow—the fact that Scripture includes dreams as a means by which godly messages can be conveyed to us. It is hard to believe that this is not just superstitious nonsense reserved for desert nomads; to accept that the biblical writers just might have known, intuitively, a great deal more about the working of the subconscious than we have hitherto suspected. Yet we must participate in this basic attitude change, to begin to feel comfortable with some other conclusions from Scripture regarding dreams.

How do we know whether to pay attention to a dream or to chalk it up to an overdose of pizza "with everything," devoured the night before? I do not pretend to be a dream analyst, nor do I want to be, but there are some helpful clues regarding this "dark speech" that have been beneficial to me.

In chapter 41 of Genesis, we find the record of Pharaoh's dream, in which he watched seven fat cows devoured by seven lean cows and seven full ears of corn devoured by seven thin. We read that "in the morning his spirit was troubled . . ." (v. 8). One of the signals by which we can know that these "books written in a foreign tongue" are to be observed is a feeling of being disturbed.

The dream lingers during the day. It tromps upon our wakeful hours. We wonder what it meant or why it came. We are upset, dismayed, or distressed. Very likely, then, we can conclude that these symbols are not just the result of interior ruminations, but are messages we should attempt to understand.

A repetition of our dreams, a pattern, a series dealing with the same subject, a similarity of themes playing over a period of time—days, months, years—is an indicator that this dream needs our attention. Pharaoh dreamed the same dream twice, in different forms, for the sake of emphasis. When we don't pay attention to the tidy housekeeper throwing up a message from the subconscious, she often finds it necessary to repeat her efforts, sometimes in a slightly different symbol.

To pay attention to a dream does not mean sitting ourselves down and stewing about the dreadful happening in our subconscious. No, it means "loving the question itself," recognizing it to be a locked room—a foreign language book—and *being gently patient*. It does not mean holding unctuous parlor conversations beginning with, "I had the strangest dream last night. . . ." It does mean sitting back, calmly and quietly, and realizing with Joseph that the interpretations of these communications are not often in our power to grasp, but that the Holy Spirit is always the interpreter of our dreams. "It is not in me: God shall give Pharaoh an answer of peace."

We learn to pray regarding these disturbers, "Lord, give me the interpretation, the hidden meaning in this symbolic message."

A few other tidbits of information regarding dreams, and then we are done with the first of the tidy housekeeper's methods of communication. Many dream analysts feel that a large percentage of our dreams are about ourselves, even when we dream of other people. A friend said to me recently, "I dreamed that my husband married another woman. Right in front of me. She was beautiful, too!"

My approach to a dream of that nature would be to first examine what it is about myself that I was dreaming. It would not be a case for examining my husband's fidelity, but for asking, "What is this dream telling me about myself? What part of myself does the other woman symbolize?" I might discover that the dream was not about my husband marrying another woman, but rather about him wedding another part of my own woman. I might discover that the beautiful bride was myself!

Another thing to remember is that dreams generally have two levels. There is the obvious interpretation, some event that happened yesterday and which we dreamed about last night; then there is the hidden, more essential meaning. Perhaps the dream of my friend was not about her relationship with her husband, but was a symbol of her relationship with her spiritual Bridegroom, her Lord. We have to wait upon the Interpreter of dreams to teach us the obvious as well as the deeper meanings. Often that takes a little time.

When I started to write, after a passage of deeper spiritual growth, I had to wait for years to receive the full interpretation of one dream of mine. In the dream, I had been traveling with a group of companions in what I can only call the heavenlies. We were journeying through the skies, surrounded by clouds. There was such an unearthly quiet there. No words were spoken, yet our communication was deep. We were close in fellowship.

After a while we descended a long, steep staircase without rails to a large convocation hall on earth, somewhere in mid-Europe. Many others had gathered before us and were waiting for a meeting to begin. I sat in a chair, and suddenly a woman near me went into labor. She was about to give birth to a child.

"Is there a doctor anywhere?" someone shouted. A doctor appeared out of the crowd. His name was Dr. Gottschaeffer. He proceeded to deliver the baby, and then to my astonishment, he turned to me with the infant and said authoritatively, "It is yours."

While I protested, the atmosphere in the hall shifted. The natural mother disappeared, the doctor vanished, and the proceedings for which everyone had been waiting began. Stunned, I wandered to the back of the hall where a long series of windows opened onto a large courtyard below. I recognized several familiar faces looking up at me. Bewildered, but becoming a little proud of the sweet bundle in my arms, I held the newborn up for viewing.

It was a dream that was particularly vivid, one that troubled me. "Lord," I prayed, "give me the interpretation." The obvious meaning was made clear right away.

I had been suffering from a case of classic writer's block. A deadline loomed on a major project, but I seemed powerless to finish it because much of what I wanted to write had been taught to me by other women, my spiritual mothers. Each time I sat at the typewriter, I was plagued by fears of being a wanton plagiarist.

Originality has always demanded my premium respect. I hate doing anything, creatively, that other people have done before me, and I suppose that the block was partly caused by this. Mostly, I believe, it was due to my reluctance to steal anyone else's thunder.

"The baby is yours," said the Deliverer of life. Another woman had given birth to it, but it was mine to display to the people standing outside. I know virtually nothing about the German language, but I was aware that the word for God is *Gott*. God was the Deliverer of life who had pronounced that the baby, my current infant of creativity, was my own child after all. "It is yours," he had repeated.

Understanding even that much of the dream freed me. Happily, I finished the project, the worrisome roadblock no longer detouring my progress.

A couple of years after the dream, I received a deeper interpretation. I had a chance to share it with one of the women who had taught me so much. She was visiting in our town, staying with a friend who happened to be a German professor. It wasn't long after we said our goodbyes that I received a phone call from her. She had been sharing my dream with her friend.

"Karen," she asked excitedly, "do you know the full meaning of that doctor's name?"

I had been right. *Gott*, in German, means God. What I hadn't known was that the word *schaeffer* means creator. The baby wasn't really mine or anyone else's. It is God who is the Creator and Deliverer of all life. The baby was really his to give. We only discover and convey his truth, truth that already exists, to those around us.

I am learning to respect the symbolic language of the subconscious, and since I believe that the tidy housekeeper fussing in the rooms of our souls is a superintendent appointed by the Creator of that soul himself, I naturally take it for granted that these special dreams have something to do with God. A part of me needs altering, cleaning, healing. He wants me to know about it. This dark language is a clue from him to help me discover what is unfinished, blocked in me. If I listen carefully enough, without becoming obsessed with subjective messages, I may even understand when they are commands to obedience.

Another way the tidy housekeeper captures the attention of the will, when we refuse to take care of the dirty laundry buried in our household, is through producing erratic behavior.

Have you ever found yourself suddenly flaring at someone toward whom you had no real reason to bear anger? Perhaps you have come home and wondered, "Now why did I get so angry with him?" You have simply experienced transferred anger, an erratic type of behavior. You were not really angry at that husband or friend or child. It was something that person said or did that reminded you of a similar painful incident locked into the subconscious, a happening in the past that had once caused you pain.

Depression, self-hatred, unreasonable intolerances—

these are all means by which she waves down our attention. They are unpleasant devices, to say the least. They can become dangerous if they begin to consume us, perhaps resulting in progressive emotional illness—and none of us want to experience that. Yet I wonder if it wouldn't be better to view them as God's good gifts, temporary uncomfortable means by which he gains our attention. He uses them to notify us that all is not well in our souls, that something within needs help if we are to be made whole.

These discomforting conditions are usually symptoms of a deeper, hidden illness, and I think one of the quickest ways to understand what is going on within is to pray, "Lord, you are the Creator of the subconscious. You are the Guardian of it. Teach me what it is you want me to know. Help me to understand the disease from which these symptoms spring."

Once we have recognized these kinds of behavior for what they are, once we have prayed the prayer, we must discipline ourselves to listen. The locked doors open slowly; the foreign language may be interpreted painfully. We may need to seek the help of a wise counselor.

The last and often final means to which the persistent cleaning woman turns is physical illness or psychosomatic pain. Medical science is beginning to *deal* with a fact that it has *recognized* for years, that there is an interrelationship between the body and the spirit. Many clinics are establishing a holistic approach to psychological treatment. They wisely realize the frustrations of dichotomizing between these parts of man. Physical healing is often a state of mind. Emotional healing is often a state of body.

For us, seeking to gain clues to our own subconscious condition, there is a need to recognize certain physical distresses for what they truly are. How ashamed we become when someone whispers the word *psychosomatic*. Wouldn't an attitude of "Hm-m-m-m, how interesting" be better? If this is a clue, if this pain (this headache, stomach cramp, burning, dizziness) is an indicator of some deep turmoil within me, how lucky I am! What kind of intriguing possibilities of self-knowledge lie ahead?

We need to be grateful that our bodies are so intertwined with our spirits, that they do begin to malfunction when all is not well. There is no cause for shame, but for simple recognition that the material part of me is intimately related to the emotional part of me.

A young man who had been undergoing a great deal of stress recently called me on the phone. His romance had been on again, off again. "Do you think I could be having some psychosomatic symptoms?" he inquired, then went on to describe some physical difficulties he had been experiencing.

Because we were close, I knew a great deal about his past. There was a history of parental child abuse, of alcoholism. My friend, I knew, had a subconscious longing for a stable father figure. The intriguing thing about his comments was that he communicated a great deal of emotional pain, but his prayers to God (his Heavenly Father) were particularly controlled. It was as though he didn't want to risk losing his spiritual Father's favor by being honest about his emotional feelings. I sensed that he was very angry with God.

"Have you told God what you feel about him?" (Anger that God had allowed this woman to come into his life, one of a series of women who had loved, then withheld her love; anger that God had not kept him from falling in love. Fear that God would never bring anyone into his life who would love him the way he needed to be loved. Distress at the thought that maybe he was unworthy of love. A feeling of being used by God because he had been trying so hard to be righteous, to be obedient.)

"No," he replied.

I recommended he try what my mother calls "the prayer of ventilation," getting off our chests, all those negative feelings that we foolishly try to hide from God, who knows them anyway. He followed my advice and reported a rather extended session of ranting and raving. The symptoms that had been distressing him disappeared and did not recur. This young man had simply been storing too much in the locked rooms of his soul, afraid of offending his Heavenly Father. He had been working hard to achieve God's love through his model spiritual behavior.

The subconscious was at work again. My friend was wise enough to recognize it.

Dreams, erratic behavior, pain—these are some of the methods by which the subconscious seeks to win the attention of the conscious mind. These are means by which our housekeeper shouts "Here! Get rid of this!" regarding the guilt buried in our souls, or the pain of another's sin against us that has boarded the doors of our hearts. "Here!" she insists in a flash of memory, a stab of grief, a bewildering emotional outburst. "Get rid of this filthy thing! I don't want it around here anymore!"

The glorious message of Redemption, which many of us have forgotten, or which many of us don't understand, is that Christ has come to save us from our sins, from the sins we have committed against him and against others, from the guilt that locks the rooms of our souls. He has come to free us from the results of the sins of others against us.

He can spring open these jailed hearts. He can enter locked rooms. That is what the act of Calvary is all about. That is what the message of Scripture proclaims. He can heal us from our distress. He can deliver us from the sin that binds us. He is willing to forgive us our errors. He has made atonement for our misdeeds. He is longing to free us from the past that enslaves us, to open us to love. He has come to restore our innocence, to create again our infinite capacity to embrace.

It is a mansion he is seeking to build in our souls—a palace, a temple, a manor. He wants to reign in the habitation of the heart, to dwell in countless unexplored pavilions and terraces and grand halls. He wants us to discover that the more love we give away, the more room there is to love. The architecture of a sacred structure is being formed in our souls.

LIFE RESPONSE

In order to identify the messages being tossed up from the subconscious, we must begin to recognize them for what they are, then make a deliberate effort to understand them. Several suggestions might be helpful:

Keep a dream diary. Place a notebook by your bedside to record the language of the subconscious that seems important. Many of us insist that we can't remember our dreams. But if we will not hop out of bed in the morning, but rather rest quietly for a few minutes, it will be surprising how much will come back to us. Jot down what you remember. Then make an effort to identify any patterns. Inquire of the Lord; ask him to give you understanding.

Trace any aberrant behavior to its source. Never allow yourself to become angry or get depressed without making some effort to answer the question, "What caused this?" Most of us are helpless before our emotions because we have never disciplined ourselves to understand the source of our feelings. Consequently, we respond only to extreme circumstances, like the straw that breaks the camel's back. It's not the straw we need to come to terms with, but all the baggage beneath it. "Why am I so angry? Why was I so hateful?" are important questions that aid our emotional maturity. Deal with the luggage, not the straw.

Notice any patterns in chronic painful conditions. Granted, there are many ailments that demand medical aid; but other physical complaints, such as a headache that regularly occurs before family gatherings, merit our wise consideration because of their regularity. Is there a pattern to my pain? Does it come before similar events? If so, this may be a clue to take into account during the reading of subconscious messages.

Do you
wince when you hear his name
made vanity?

What if you were not so safe
sheltered, circled by love
and convention?
What if
the world shouted at you?
Could you take the string
of hoarse words—glutton,
wino, devil, crazy
man, agitator, . . .
nigger-lover, rebel,
and hang the grimy ornament
around your neck
and answer
love?

See the sharp stones poised
against your head! even
your dear friend
couples your name with curses
("By God! I know not God!")
the obscene affirmation
of infidelity
echoes, insistent,
from a henhouse roof.

Then—Slap! Spit! the whip,
the thorn. The gravel
grinds your fallen knees
under a whole world's weight
until
the hammering home of all

your innocence
stakes you, stranded,
halfway between hilltop and heaven
(neither will have you).

And will you whisper
forgive?

"THE REVOLUTIONARY"
Luci Shaw

FIVE
Huntsman at the Door

One afternoon last fall a blue flash in the gnarled oak tree caught my eye. *Oh, good!* I thought. *The jays are back.* Then the color soared beyond my boxed-in, window vision.

I rushed downstairs to see if the bird had been attracted by the corn kernels in my son's newly made feeder. (I am the official bird recorder in our family. Since I am home the most, I have been assigned the responsibility of keeping track of which birds land at which stations, what time of day they arrive, and which foods they prefer. This is all dutifully charted in a notebook that will eventually determine our entire feeding philosophy!)

The jay was not at the feeder, but the cocker spaniel was at the back door, so I let her out and stepped outside myself to watch her bound through the brush of the woods, an animal motion that I love.

My attention was turned to two little birds who had become trapped in our screened-in porch. The door had fallen off last spring and had not been replaced. A vireo had beaten herself to death in this prison chamber earlier in the year. We had found her flying frantically against the mesh screening. The children and I had tried to catch her in order to set her free, but she would not be caught until it was too late and she had bludgeoned herself with hopeless flights and desperate falls. Finally we had placed her on the picnic table, hoping she would gather strength to fly away, but the breath had slowly ebbed from her brushed-yellow breast.

Now, here was a chickadee flailing for freedom; there was a thrush. If only they would find the access they had entered, but they kept throwing themselves against the opaque screens, wondering, I suppose, at the free air that seemed so near and yet was so elusive. The black-capped chickadee was more assertive than the thrush. He banged and flapped, his little beak open with fright. I hoped he had not ruptured himself already. The tweed-coated thrush was more resigned, sensing perhaps, the danger of challenging any walls, whether mesh or concrete.

I knew I could never catch them with my bare hands. The terror of my touch would be a certain death sentence. Poor birds—not only were they imprisoned, but here was a huntsman set loose upon them as well. "O God," I breathed, "help me to set them free without hurting them." If He cared for the common sparrow, He must also be concerned for the thrush and the chickadee.

I finally found a bucket and tried to capture them, but

64

the chickadee rolled in the air, landed against the prison walls, and hung for a moment upside down, his claws entangled in the screen. My heart stopped. A fall would be fatal.

This emboldened my shy efforts and I bucketed the chickadee, slipped a piece of the children's cardboard puppet theater (this summer's project) between the container and the screen, carried all outside, and watched the dauntless bird dash off into the woods.

Next, the thrush. Her tail fanned against the screen, a dun-and gray-colored spray as she hopped before me. But finally, she too was between the board and the bucket, and I released her. Stunned, she tumbled onto the grass, her heart in wild percussion—just as the cocker came bounding back from woody haunts.

"Hurry, thrush!" I warned. "No sense escaping prison only to land in the cocker's soft mouth." She flew!

This must be the way it is with us. We flail in the prison of our souls, beating ourselves to death like the chickadee, or waiting resignedly for the end like the thrush. The Huntsman comes to set us free, to pinion us for a moment, in order to release us into the world we see dimly beyond the spirit's screens. We fly before him, evading the terror of his grasp, refusing to believe it is for our own good that he hunts us.

Through no doing of our own, we are entrapped. Because of our instinctive inheritance, none of our hearts are completely free. Unlike the birds, however, we sin because we have the power to welcome the Huntsman, and instead, we refuse him access. We close our cages, preferring to bang within them. Terrorized, we listen to the knocking at the door. The Huntsman pounds. He sits waiting on the mat. Ever a gentleman, he refuses to transgress the boundaries we have established, but in his love he even slips a key of freedom through the bars.

That key will unlock these cells if only we will accept it, push it into the lock. We refuse. In essence, we thrust the key back. This is our rebellion, this preferring the prison chamber. Now our imprisonment becomes our own doing. We bear responsibility for our trapped condition.

The key, of course, is forgiveness, God's offering of pardon for our basic human rebellion, our refusal of his original intent for our lives. One day we must all come to terms with that key shoved under the door. We can refuse God's act of initiating love. We can pretend it isn't there. We can waste ourselves⁻ with fruitless substitutes—or we can pick up the key, push it into the lock, turn the tumblers, and open the door.

Then he, God of the universe, personal Creator, the One who will eventually fill all places, comes into our restricted habitations. He sups with us, communes with us—and immediately begins the business of creating a mansion in our souls.

It is interesting to note that the human soul demands its atonement—that is what all the beating and flailing is about. Paul Tournier, the noted psychiatrist, in his book *Guilt and Grace*, explains it this way:

Numerous illnesses, both physical and nervous, and even accidents, or frustrations in social or professional life are revealed by psychoanalysis to be attempts at the expiation of guilt which is wholly unconscious. It is a form of punishment which the sufferer administers to himself, and it goes on repeating itself indefinitely with a kind of inexorable fatality. They attempt—vainly, and unconsciously, to be sure—to make expiation, to "pay." And they do pay, quite literally, with their health.

What a sentence we are under—hapless humanity,

doomed to undergo an endless expiation for the sins we have committed. We cannot bear our guilt.

"The weight of guilt is so intolerable," writes Tournier again, "that everyone shows this self-justificatory reflex which modern psychology speaks of as the repression of the conscience, that is to say the repression of guilt into the unconscious, out of the field of consciousness."

The conscious mind cannot bear the remembrance of its own shameful acts. It pushes the thought of them down into the vault of the subconscious. But the tidy housekeeper throws her discoveries back to the conscious mind. When the conscious mind redoubles its efforts, the subconscious redoubles hers. She communicates via dreams, erratic behavior, pain. The soul is demanding expiation.

The basic premise of the gospel is that we have sinned. We have fallen short of God's standard. We have become something less than what he intended us to be. We bear true guilt for our misdeeds. We have become damaged because of our sins. Helpless to undo what has been done, we need One to redeem our mistakes.

If we do not accept his atonement, we will ever make unsatisfactory atonement for ourselves.

Christ is the One who redeems us from our endless rounds of expiations. He has become the atonement for us.

Surely he has borne our griefs
   and carried our sorrows . . .
But he was wounded for our transgressions,
   he was bruised for our iniquities;
upon him was the chastisement that made us whole,
   and with his stripes we are healed.
All we like sheep have gone astray;
   we have turned every one to his own way;

and the Lord has laid on him
the iniquity of us all.

Isaiah 53:4-6

What a marvelous reprieve has been provided by the Creator! There is no need to spin out life in this never-ending atonement-making. Christ has offered to be the expiation. He has willingly become the atonement our psyches demand. He has become sin for us.

Our skeptical world scoffs at sin and guilt. It decries the need for supernatural grace—*but it participates in the endless cycle of subconscious expiation, just the same.* Man suffers from true guilt whether he calls it parental pressures, societal expectations, or whatever. Unwittingly, he is a player in the drama of atonement, despite the words he chooses to explain away reality. Modern philosophies are not necessarily true just because they are modern.

We cannot appreciate atonement, we cannot fathom forgiveness until we understand how far we have come from what we once were. Our remembrance of that long-ago beginning is dimmed. Perhaps it has become a part of everyman's subconscious experience. Thus we continually long for Edens, long without understanding why.

This was the purpose of the incarnation, of Christ taking on human flesh. It was to remind us of what the Father intended each of us to be. Jesus was the demonstration of things past, of lost Edens, and of things present, everyman's potential now.

"Love your enemy. Don't commit adultery even in your heart. Don't resist attacks. Do your good deeds privately. Pray in your closet. Don't be consumed with material concerns. Make the spiritual primary in your life. Never criticize or condemn. Be concerned more with your own faults"—all these were revolutionary teachings propounded by a man who, unlike most teachers, was able to live what he taught.

"Love your God with all your heart, soul, mind, and strength. Love your neighbor as yourself." This was the cornerstone of his pedagogy.

Then this man went on to demonstrate by his life, by his miracles, that he was who he claimed to be, sent from God, indeed God incarnate.

"Are you really the One we are waiting for, or shall we keep on looking?" was the question John asked.

Christ's reply was a verification of his authenticity: "Go back to John and tell him all you have seen and heard here today: how those who were blind can see! The lame are walking without a limp! The lepers are completely healed! The deaf can hear again! And the poor are hearing the Good News!" Christ was the new Adam.

He showed us how to live, how to have power over sin—our own or those of others against us. Ultimately, he laid down his life for his friends (the whole world). He was what we were all intended to be. Atonement takes on perspective when we see how far we have all come from Creation.

Just as there are two levels of sin that have closed our hearts—our own and others' against us—so there are two levels of forgiveness with which we must deal. We must experience forgiveness for our own sins, that massive primary rebellion of refusing to be united with God. And on this first level, we require forgiveness for the daily, cumulative shortcomings of living that tend to separate us from him as well. The first level springs from God to us, and better enables us to approach the second level of forgiveness—forgiving those who have sinned against us. This spirit of peace then emanates from us to those around us.

Forgiveness is always contingent upon our confession. "If we confess our sins, he is faithful and just, and will forgive our sins and cleanse us from all unrighteousness" (1 John 1:9).

And the human attitude that enables us to confess is the attitude of repentance. We must intend to turn from our willful flailing in the prison. We have gained a vision of what we can become. There is an inkling of understanding that we cannot be what we want to be without help. We are sorry for pushing the key back, for keeping the Huntsman waiting on the mat. We confess where it is that we have erred.

On a purely psychological level, confession is a powerful therapeutic device. The old saying, "Confession is good for the soul," is amazingly true. It is a hose turned on the filthy interiors of our dusty, boarded rooms. It is a powerful cleansing agent.

Confession before God, our Wise Counselor, is the catharsis necessary to receive his offered forgiveness. This catharsis is a sudden flash of awful self-knowledge. It is coming to terms with the awesome truth of who we really are. It is a verbal symbol of emotional release—we are no longer holding our guilt, our pain, our grief to ourselves. It is acknowledging the messages of the tidy housekeeper. It is turning the handle to the closet door, opening up the room, and showing it to the One waiting outside. It is pointing, "There, there is the dirt. This is what I shoved into the cupboard. Here is what I hid under the couch."

God always accepts our confessions. He never points a finger and clucks, "Tsk-tsk." He never reacts with horror or outrage. He never turns his back on us. His response is *always* love. He receives into himself the awful confessions of the soul. He forgives.

Confession names the terrible things, points them out.

Forgiveness trundles them away, out of sight, *out of mind.* "I have swept away your transgressions like a cloud, and your sins like mist; return to me, for I have redeemed you" (Isa. 44:22).

Private confession should be one of the regular disciplines of the Christian life. "I have sinned, O Father. I have sinned." We should examine our conscience daily and discover what is there that might hinder our intimate communion with God. Are we pulling shades over the windows again? Are we beginning to board rooms?

This is not a morbid exercise. It must not become a fascination with the dysfunction of self. It should be an established habit that we undertake in order to once again experience joy. The soul loves so to be released from guilt, to be unboarded again.

There are some sins that the subconscious has stored so long, it cannot believe there is any relief for them. The subconscious needs to be convinced. It needs to hear the words, "You are forgiven."

When you have prayed privately, confessing your sin time and again, and when you do not experience release, it is time to call on the ministry of the Body of Christ. This is one of the functions for which God has provided the community of believers. Someone has to pronounce the words of forgiveness. Our soul needs a little convincing.

Seek out a trusted Christian counselor, a spiritual advisor who is intimate with God, a friend who is growing spiritually and who loves you. Explain that you can't find release from your guilt through your own prayers. Remind the person of the necessity of complete confidence. Tell him/her how you have sinned. Ask that person to repeat firmly the words from 1 John, "If you confess your sins, he is faithful and just to forgive you your sins, and to cleanse you from all unrighteousness" (v. 9).

Have the person say to you the words our Lord was so

ready to use (and which always stirred the anger of the religious authorities), "Child, your sins are forgiven thee." The subconscious will believe when these words are said by a believer. This in no way denigrates Christ's adequacy. It only means that someone must be Christ's mouth to the lamed soul. Someone must say the wonderful words, "You are forgiven!" in a human audible voice so they can be heard spiritually.

We look to Christ to see what the Creator intended us to be. We then look into our boarded interiors and realize how badly we need forgiveness. The only remedy is to throw ourselves prone and confess how short we are of the mark.

God's forgiveness is the key that unlocks all doors shut by our own guilt. Christ's work of redemption at Calvary was not just a work for that era, but a work for all time. His cry, "Father, forgive them, for they know not what they do!" was not just a cry for then, but a shout for today. Christ's atonement was not just for the individual, for the private subconscious storing a load of repressed guilt. It is an expiation for the corporate consciousness, for the mass mind, for mankind.

His Calvary is the cross that has cracked eternity.

The Hater cringed to hear the sound he feared above all else. The doorway of the worlds stood open. He felt the giant key that dangled from his belt. He wished to gloat a little longer in his victory but left the silent gallows where the Singer was as dead as the rotting beams of the machine.
He reached the threshold of eternity and found the doorway of the worlds not only open but clearly ripped away. He strained to hear the everlasting wail, the eternal dying which he loved. All was silent. Then he heard the Song.

"No," he cried. "Give me back the door and key for this is my domain." He felt again and found the great key at his waist had disappeared.

"Where is the key? Where is the key?" the Hater cried. But all the while the Hater knew. Each man on Terra had a key. And never could they come into the Canyon of the Damned unless they chose to do it. To live there, men would have to reject the Song.

Calvin Miller, *The Singer*

We must pick up the offered key and turn the lock, understanding, as we do so, that he will come in and sup with us and then go about the restoration of our souls. We must be prepared for the tearing down and building up, the removing of walls, the remodeling of rooms. We must be ready to choke on plaster dust, be inconvenienced by the installation of new fixtures. The Huntsman will have entered. As Master Builder, he seeks to make more room for himself.

All these are temporary inconveniences—we can overlook the discomfort. We ourselves have been freed. A key has turned in the front door. The prison has vanished. Guilt is gone. There is no more need for our subconscious to fashion its own expiations. We are becoming a habitation once more for our God. Eden is returning.

LIFE RESPONSE

Take a piece of paper and a pencil. Sit quietly and close your eyes for a while. Imagine that Christ has entered the room and has come to sit beside you. You can feel his Presence. He lays his hand on your back as you both go to prayer.

Look into your own soul. What has caused you to lock the doors of your own heart, to make this Emperor sit outside upon the mat? Do you bear guilt because of some deed you have done? Write it on the paper. Name the sin, or sins, specifically. Write a prayer of confession. Say, "Lord, I have sinned. This is the name of my sin. I want so much to be rid of it. Forgive me, I pray."

In prayer, with your eyes closed, imagine your sin as a bundle of dirty rags. Roll the bundle into a tight wad. Tie it with a length of string. Hand it to Christ who is close beside you. Watch now as he lifts it high, high above his head. Look up in your mind's eye and see the white, shimmering throne of God. Watch as the bundle, your sins, disappears from the hands of Jesus, is incinerated in the great heat of that consuming fire.

Now read the words of the following statement. Supply your name in the blank. Keep the Presence of Christ close in your imagination. Perhaps you can hear him saying the words; he has said them so many times before.

My child, _____ , your sins are forgiven. If you confess your sins, I am faithful and just to forgive you your sins, and to cleanse you from all unrighteousness. My child, your sins are forgiven.

I shall never forgive him
My stubborn heart cried—
Until I remembered
    You taught us forgiveness
    Hanging on the aweful tree
    And now You whisper
    As You see me nailed
    By prejudice and grudges
    Roman-soldiered
    By an unforgiving spirit
    To my own small tree:
It is never forgiveness until you forgive
the impossible to forgive . . .
    And in the forgiving—
    No matter the measure of hurting—
    My spirit, with Yours, is set free!

    "FORGIVENESS, ANOTHER WORD FOR LOVE"
                                Wilma Burton

SIX
The Key
That Unlocks Doors

Shakespeare's works are often studies in revenge,
dramatic examples of the corroding process of bitterness,
the creeping horror of vengeance. Recently, my husband
and I attended a performance of *Richard the Third*. We
both noticed the lines of the mourning queens, whose
husbands, sons, and brothers had all been murdered by
the tyrant king.

Queen Elizabeth:
  O thou, well skill'd in curses, stay awhile
  And teach me how to curse mine enemies.
Queen Margaret:
  Forbear to sleep the night, and fast the day;
  Compare dead happiness with living woe;

Think that thy babes were sweeter than they were,
And he that slew them fouler than he is:
Bettering thy loss makes the bad causer worse:
Revolving this will teach thee how to curse.

This is the natural tendency of humanity: upon being wronged by a fellow human, we nurse our grievances, we nurture our offense, we feed upon our hatred, we "better our losses, revolving them." Reprisal is as native to the human condition as respiration.

Something untoward occurs to us, however, when we return evil for evil, when we allow bitterness to burrow in our souls, we become imprinted with the deformed emblem of Richard III, our emotional bodies become twisted, crippled.

What's more, when our grievance grows to hatred, we become slaves of the very persons we hate. We are bound to them with chains that leave us no moments of peace. Waking, we are haunted by their presence. Our sleeping is shadowed by their deeds. Our memories are clouded by their wrongdoing. Their present actions grind and gore us. We have allowed hatred to become our incarceration.

Another natural human response, other than vengeance, is to close ourselves off from any more pain. We seclude ourselves from further blows, rummage in some hideout in our souls, then pull the door behind us. The results of this activity are also damaging. There is no door we can close in our hearts without risky effects. We chance blocking out God's love, or shutting ourselves away from cherished human love.

Christ's forgiveness toward the mallet-pounders, toward those who wove torture-thorns, toward those who insultingly shot spit into his eyes, toward the sadistic ones who enjoyed his suffering—Christ's forgiveness toward those who wronged him is a model for our forgiveness.

(Oh! how could they break those hands that healed the gnarled hands of others? How misuse the flesh that God himself had cherished—*this is my beloved!* From what jaundiced audacity did they spit into his eyes when he had used his own spittle to make a paste so that another man might see! How did they laugh at agony! How enjoy pain-breath dying! *"Father, forgive them, for they know not what they do!"*)

The first level of forgiveness with which we must become proficient is personal forgiveness received from God for the errors *we* have committed before him. The second level should be directed toward those who have wronged *us*. There is much explicit instruction in the Scriptures regarding this second type of discipline.

In the Lord's Prayer, that teaching guide Christ gave to his disciples, we notice the phrase ". . . and forgive us our debts, as we also have forgiven our debtors." Christ elaborates on this statement in Matthew, "For if you forgive men their trespasses, your heavenly Father also will forgive you; but if you do not forgive men their trespasses, neither will your Father forgive your trespasses" (6:14,15).

In Matthew 18 Christ stresses the tale of the unforgiving servant. The whole parable is worth our attention.

Therefore the kingdom of heaven may be compared to a king who wished to settle accounts with his servants. When he began the reckoning, one was brought to him who owed him ten thousand talents; and as he could not pay, his lord ordered him to be sold, with his wife and children and all that he had, and payment to be made. So the servant fell on his knees, imploring him, "Lord, have patience with me, and I will pay you everything." And out of pity for him the lord of that servant released him and forgave him the debt. But that same servant, as he went out, came upon one of his fellow servants who owed him a hundred denarii; and seizing him by the throat he said, "Pay what you owe." So his fellow servant fell down and besought him, "Have patience with me, and I will pay you." He refused and went and put him in prison till he should pay the debt. When his fellow servants saw what had taken place, they were greatly distressed, and they went and reported to their lord all that had taken place. Then his lord summoned him and said to him, "You wicked servant! I forgave you all that debt because you besought me; and should not you have had mercy on your fellow servant, as I had mercy on you?" And in anger his lord delivered him to the jailers, till he should pay all his debt. So also my heavenly Father will do to every one of you, if you do not forgive your brother from your heart (vv. 23-35).

Mark 11:25, 26 reads, "And whenever you stand praying, forgive, if you have anything against any one; so that your Father also who is in heaven may forgive you your trespasses."

Colossians 3:12 states, "Put on then, as God's chosen ones, holy and beloved, compassion, kindness, lowliness, meekness, and patience, forbearing one another and, if one has a complaint against another, forgiving each other; as the Lord has forgiven you, so you also must forgive."

Undeniably, Scripture teaches that God's forgiveness for us is conditional upon our willingness to forgive those around us, those who have wronged ourselves. I think the best way to understand these many Scripture verses is to avoid casting God in the role of the manipulating overseer who refuses our broken and contrite cries when we fail (he is not nearly as performance-oriented as we suppose he is).

It is more helpful in attempting to understand the meaning of these passages to return to the analogy of the household of our subconscious. We must remind ourselves that God looks upon our hearts. He is cognizant of our interior habitations. He knows full well when we have boarded a part of ourselves, when we have padlocked pain, when we have drawn shades and drapes. We need to think of God's contingent forgiveness not so much in terms of him being *unwilling* to forgive when we refuse to do our work of forgiveness, as his being *unable* to forgive us. Just as he refuses to transgress the locked doors of our hearts, so he restrains himself from violating the interior structure of our souls. When we refuse to turn the key of forgiveness in regard to others, we block his sweeping power of forgiveness in our own hearts.

What is forgiveness? I think I found the best definition in a Bible dictionary years ago. "Forgiveness is being willing to bear the pain of another's misdeeds against us."

This is truly amazing! To bear the pain of another's misdeed—to be willing to bear the rejection of a husband's sexual infidelity? To be willing to bear the physical abuse of a parent's beating? To be willing to bear the emotional agony of another's malicious verbal slander? To be willing to bear the humiliation of a child's sowing of rank, wild seeds? To be willing to bear the pain?

Yes, forgiveness means that we must bring our wills into obedience with the commands in Scripture regarding forgiving those who have caused us pain. God has given us responsibility for the tip of the iceberg of our mind, the will. This is the area we must laboriously push into proper position. We must grapple it to a point of acquiescence. "Uncle!" it must cry. "I am willing to bear the pain!"

Forgiveness is costly. It is an agony of submission. It is often entered into with tears. But it is only when we are willing to accept the sacrifice of suffering another offers to us that we can truly understand Christ's extravagant venture of forgiveness.

We must be willing to bear the pain. Then we will know how Christ walked into the court of the High Priest, into the council of Herod, into the presence of Pilate, into the jeering madness of the streets of Jerusalem, onto the hill beyond the city. He walked willingly. Willingly he bore the misdeeds against himself committed by a grotesque, perverted, and insane world. "Father, forgive them . . ." was his cry. We must learn to make it ours.

Each time we forgive, we are participating slightly in the all-inclusive suffering of Christ.

Once we have brought the will into submission, we have done our part. It is God's responsibility to free the mysterious, complicated, evasive subconscious.

Forgiveness must be offered even when it has not been requested. Somehow we have adopted the pious attitude that we will forgive when the offending party comes begging for our forgiveness. That must be done, of course, but that is such an impractical idea, because the beggars rarely come! I have been sinned against mightily (so have you—we have also offended) and rarely has anyone implored my forgiveness. Most of them don't even know they have wronged me. Another's sins against me can be overt or covert. They can be real or imagined.

None of Christ's persecutors stood at the foot of his cross pleading for pardon. Yet the Lord's pronouncement was gasped out magnanimously, painfully, willingly, "Father, forgive them . . ."

Forgiveness must be offered again and again. It becomes a daily prayer, "How have I sinned? Forgive me, Lord. Who has sinned against me? Lord, I forgive." Peter came to the Lord, I suspect a little smugly, and asked, "Lord, how often shall my brother sin against me, and I forgive him? As many as seven times?" Christ's reply was, "Seven times seventy." According to my calculations, that was 490 times.

I may have been sinned against a great deal—but no one has sinned against me that often! Yet this is Christ's endless expectation, a practice he has perfected—we must learn to forgive again and again.

Scripture teaches that we must forgive those who have sinned against us. We recognize that God's ability to forgive us on the primary level, for our own misdeeds, is often conditional upon our own acts of forgiveness. So we understand that forgiveness is the willingness to bear the pain of another's misdeeds against us. We have come to terms with the fact that we must forgive without being asked, that we may have to utter our prayers over and over. Now what?

Now we must learn to wait for God to touch the subconscious. Forgiveness is an act of the will that waits until God has released the emotion. We control the conscious mind that recognizes the need of the subconscious; but it is God who performs the miracles of opening closed doors and cleansing the rooms behind them. How often I have marched into my bedroom, gone down to my knees, and prayed, "I forgive. I forgive. Now I refuse to leave here until you have done the work of forgiveness in my soul."

I believe the words, "To err is human; *to forgive divine.*" It is impossible for us to *experience* forgiveness without some kind of supernatural intervention. Even forgiveness on the second level, for those who have sinned against us, requires godly quickening if we are to benefit from its full effects. We are dependent upon a spiritual intermediary. Our obedient wills are not enough.

We will know that we have forgiven, that we have experienced the results of forgiveness, when we can look back on what used to cause us pain with no more torment. We will know that God has touched us when the past is reconciled, when hatred dies.

Then another mysterious work of redemption occurs. When we say we are willing to bear the pain of another's misdeed against us, when we pronounce the words, "I forgive," Christ draws the grief, the disease, the chagrin, the suffering, the damage unto himself! Christ in his atonement took upon himself all of this world's sin, that of the past, that of the present, that of the future, that of the one who has erred against you. He becomes our reconciliation.

Let us be careful to wait for God's work within us. It is easy to fall into the old human trap of making our own expiations. Our responsibility is to be willing to bear the pain. It is God who accomplishes the work, the release of forgiveness.

Just as the subconscious needs a little convincing in order to receive God's personal forgiveness, often it needs a little persuasion that we have forgiven others. Again, this is one of the reasons Christ called a spiritual community together. We often need to hear the words that Christ would speak reassuring us: "Now you have forgiven."

If we have forgiven and forgiven, yet do not experience psychological release, we need to turn again to a trusted Christian counselor, a pastor, a friend, or spouse. Let us confess our own sinful attitudes resulting from the friction of another's life against ours, then let us ask the

84

other believer to hear our prayers of forgiveness, "I forgive . . ."

The counselor will pray the words firmly: "In the name of Jesus Christ, and on his behalf, I am a witness to that fact that you have forgiven _____ for his sins against you. You are willing to bear the pain. If Christ was here, he would say the words (I only say them in his behalf), 'You have forgiven.' He is doing the work of forgiveness in your soul. Amen."

It is lovely to think that one of the major concerns of the Lord when he appeared after his resurrection to those waiting in the upper room was this concern that we would experience the release of forgiveness. "Receive the Holy Spirit. If you forgive the sins of any, they are forgiven; if you retain the sins of any, they are retained" (John 20:23). We must learn not to bind people's sins to them by retaining those sins, but we must go about the ministry of releasing ourselves and one another, through forgiveness. This is part of the work of the body, "Confess your sins to one another," writes James "that you may be healed" (5:16).

A friend and I once tangled on the role of women in the church. Since I was a woman and he was a man, we brought opposing views to our supposedly objective discussions. Interpreting biblical passages differently, both of us thought our own views to be correct. Heatedly, we argued toe to toe, nose to nose. Unintentionally, without malice, his words became a battering ram. (I have no idea what mine became to him.) Every once in a while, I still discover surprising remnant bruises from our encounters.

I forgave and forgave, until finally I recognized that my own prayers were doing no good, and bitterness was creeping around the edges of my soul. I turned to an elder. First he listened to my confession, to the sinful attitudes and actions I felt I had committed. Then he listened to my prayers, in which I stated that I was willing to bear the pain. I would say, "Yes," to carrying those wounds in my soul. He pronounced the words, "You have forgiven." I went home free. The door in my heart that I had closed was suddenly sprung wide.

However, the relationship progressed, as well as the discussions. We were locked into a nonconciliatory settlement. The gateway to my heart was again easing shut. I strove to push it ajar. Forgiveness often demands some creativity, particularly when it is the everyday kind.

I took my prayer notebook and filled three pages with specific prayers of forgiveness. I allowed the tidy housekeeper to toss up everything she could find! On the final page, I constructed my own absolution, "In the name of the Father of all, God of very gods, before the power of the Holy Spirit, breath of life to all living, in the finished work of Christ on Calvary, and through his blood, entered mysteriously into all time, before the witness of all the saints clouding around us, I pronounce that you, Karen Mains, have forgiven. You have stated that you are willing to bear the pain. Now Christ will take that pain unto himself. God will accomplish the work of forgiveness in your soul. You are free. Amen. Amen."

It was a grand absolution! Grand, because my soul needed a little convincing. The gateway was thrown wide. It has never closed against that man to this day.

Listen! What music dances from the old house? What lights are burning in the windows? Who has thrown open the shutters, painted the porch, repaired the shingles? Who has laid a fire on the hearth, struck a match? Who has polished the knocker on the door, planted petunias?

What great celebration stirs within? Who is singing? Who are the children laughing up in the balconies? Who is practicing the piano in the parlor?

Who has planted a garden by the back door, pruned the peach trees? Who has straightened the garden gate, whitewashed the fencing?

Who is living in the old house that once stood empty in the middle of town? Whose life is filling the old place? When will the invitations to open house be sent out? Will we get a chance to see the remodeling within?

The key to forgiveness always offers the possibility of household restorations.

LIFE RESPONSE

"I am willing to bear the pain!"

I wish this next assignment could be easily undertaken, but in most cases, it will not be a simple task. Pain-bearing often hurts. But it is necessary for each of us to undergo our own small Gethsemanes.

Look over the memory review included in the Life Response section at the end of chapter two. You are basically attempting to recall who has caused you pain. Who has wounded you? Who has brought you grief? Who has sinned against you?

Begin the prayers of forgiveness. Be specific. Name the deed as well as the person. "I forgive _____ for _____ ."

You might find it helpful to write all of this down. Exercise your imagination again and visualize the Presence of Christ. This assists us in remembering that we are undertaking soul work. It also prevents us from recording bald-faced lies about our human relationships. After all, Jesus is looking over our shoulder.

Now forgive. Forgive each person for each pain.

Visualize the exchange of these griefs. Imagine Christ

taking this bundle of filth and lifting it up into the incendiary Presence of God. Jesus takes the pain from you. He discards it. See! It is gone!

Read aloud the following pronouncement:

In the name of God the Father, before the witness of the Holy Spirit, under the blood of Christ shed at Calvary, you have forgiven! The spiritual work of forgiveness is now being accomplished in your soul!

WILLIAM (Master Architect):
        We are the master-craftsmen, God and I—
        We understand one another. None, as I can,
        Can creep under the ribs of God, and feel
        His heart beat through those Six Days of Cre-
           ation;
        . . . Oh, but in making man
        God over-reached Himself and gave away
        His Godhead. He must now depend on man
        For what man's brain, creative and divine
        Can give Him. Man stands equal with Him
           now,
        Partner and rival. Say God needs a church,
        As here in Canterbury—and say He calls to-
           gether
        By miracle stone, wood and metal, builds
        A church of sorts; *my* church He cannot
           make—
        Another, but not that. This church is mine
        And none but I, not even God, can build it.

THE ZEAL OF THY HOUSE
Dorothy Sayers

SEVEN
Tower Building and Master Builders

Recently, I watched a young father attempting to help his toddler build a tower out of plastic-type blocks. The child's fat, sausage fingers were unable to manipulate the small pieces. Yet he wanted that tower built, and he wanted to build it himself. Every time the father lent what even closely resembled aid, the two year old would yell. And every time the tower wobbled and fell, he would kick his heels and yell again. After a while, we were all exhausted—child, father, and onlookers.

Parents of children of all ages frequently hear the cry, "I can do it by myself!" Whether it be building towers, using sharp scissors, clambering to a treetop house, driving a car, choosing a wife, or picking a home—this is the human being's native yelp of independence. At heart we are all conformed individualists.

Yet the child often does need help—with the scissors, the tree climb, the regulations of the highways, choosing a mate, or house-hunting. Unfortunately, few children are gifted with the wisdom to discern the proper balance between dependence and independence.

It is not just children who cry, "I can do it by myself!" Most adults choke on dependency of any kind. We strangle on the words, "I am in need, can you help me?" How bitter tasting is the phrase, "I'm hurting. Can you listen?" How tongue-tied we become when uttering, "I want to be loved."

This same I-can-do-it-myself syndrome can be transferred to the realm of the supernatural. We want to build towers, but we don't want any help. We will attempt all measures rather than admit we are dependent upon God. We have been cozened by the humanistic flattery of our time. We have swallowed the sugar-coated pill labeled Man Is Everything. We believe our systems, psychological or scientific, will reveal all, discover all, uncover all, answer all.

Without realizing it, we exalt the mannish. Subtly, we rationalize away the spiritual. Without words, we *act* as though belief in the supernatural is simply a primitive holdover. We participate in a regular rape of the natural land around us, which was not created by ourselves, and it is a symbolic violation. In a million ways, kicking our heels, screaming and thrashing, we demonstrate the cry—we can do it by ourselves!

When it comes to rebuilding the towers of the subconscious, our mysterious interior, we even dare to slip into attitudes kin to the arrogance of William, the Master Architect, reconstructing the burnt-out choir in the cathedral of Canterbury. "Oh, but in making man God over-reached Himself and gave away His Godhead. He must now depend on man for what man's brain, creative and divine can give him. Man stands equal with Him now, partner and rival."

Human builders have always strutted—"Come, let us build ourselves a city, and a tower with its top in the heaven, and let us make a name for ourselves"—but despite our braggadocio, it is not God who has over-reached himself. It is we who have the long grasps. He is not dependent upon us. Though God's love is tender in the face of our uncanny bent to evil and our incredible will to rebellion, he can function perfectly well without us.

God will never be made in man's image, no matter how we attempt to anthropomorphize. What's more, the universal truths, the life-support systems he has created, his very being, are not contingent upon our recognition. They, and he, exist whether we acknowledge it or not.

We, however, are dependent upon him. We are dependent upon the axioms he has spun into existence, upon the strands he has woven and stretched across our space-time lives, upon the structures, seen and unseen, he has crafted to bring order from chaos. It is man who is dependent upon God's web-spinning, upon his creation of eco-systems, upon his masterful healing of the sub-conscious.

He is the builder of all towers. We are only the tradesmen under his hire.

God hears our cry—"I want to do it by myself!"—and he patiently stands aside like a wise parent to see how far this temper tantrum will go, how extreme this assertiveness will become. Sometimes, again because of love, he intervenes when his knowledge reveals that our independence is leading us to ultimate disaster. We give him little credit for his emergency aid and merrily go on our way, unaltered. Then there are times when he doesn't intervene at all—and we are quick to dump all the blame on him.

Often, he scatters our proud towers. He leaves us in confusion, babbling, because it is finally time for us to learn the truth—we cannot do it by ourselves. We become like the architect in Ibsen's *The Master Builder*. Once while placing the wreath proclaiming a finished work upon a high steeple, he broke his vow to God, that of being a builder for him. "And when I stood there," states Halvard Solness, "high over everything, and was hanging the wreath over the vane, I said to him: Hear me now, thou Mighty One! From this day forward I will be a free builder—I, too in my sphere—just as thou in thine. I will never more build churches for Thee—only homes for human beings."

He never climbed the towers again, and from that time on was consumed with a fear of heights, except once—when he climbed for the wrong reason: to create a castle in the air. He fell to his death.

Remarkably, God often allows our two-year-old temper tantrums, our human doggedness, to succeed. Kindly, he honors our hearts' desires. But there comes a time in all of our lives when we are scaling a pinnacle too close to his own dominion. Here he demands that we cease the struggle, allow ourselves to be dependent, and whisper the hard words, "I need help." Suddenly, he becomes a stern and adamant parent, insisting that we come to terms with the fact that *he now wants to do it in us himself*.

Now it is easy to understand why those who do not believe in God, those who are steeped in the thinking of this post-Christian era, those who are in hot pursuit of material satisfaction, those racing after what feels good, do not recognize the existence of God. Simply, they refuse to believe that he exists.

Yet how can we account for the rank humanists in our fundamentalist, evangelical, and mainline denominational churches? They proclaim themselves to be theists, but their actions protest, "We can do it by ourselves!"

The attitude seems to be: If we *pray* hard enough, if we *work* long enough, if we *refuse* to allow what is evil in ourselves to best us, if we *struggle* desperately, if we *clench* our teeth and *hang* on with our nails, if we *want* something badly enough—then there is nothing that cannot be achieved.

I have no problem with long hours of prayer, hard work, refusing the enemy, struggling, clenching, hanging on, or wanting something badly. I have no problem, except when this process is carried on with little or no thought of God. Where is God in all this straining humanity, in all this kicking of heels, in all this energy and clamor? Is not this an echo of the old cry, "Come, let *us* build . . . let *us* make a name for ourselves . . .?" Is not this the time-worn rebellion, "I can do it by myself!"?

Aren't we transforming the ancient vehicles, the fiery chariots of God's grace, those hot wheels of prayer and spiritual longing, into modern shiny roadsters with a teenager in the driver's seat?

There is a biological phrase that describes rather well what kind of relationship with God we should be striving to achieve. The word is *symbiosis*, and it means the living together of two dissimilar organisms in close association or union, especially when this is advantageous to both.

We should be attempting to achieve symbiosis with God. How the relationship could possibly be advantageous to him is a mystery we must simply accept. But it is certainly advantageous to man. Perhaps the joining is really something deeper, something more like a synchronism, a co-inherence; but I love the idea of two dissimilar organisms joining. Can there be anything more dissimilar than the human and the divine?

In order for us to achieve this intimacy we must come to terms with all the ways in which we cry, "I want to do it myself!" We must raise our consciousness in regard to the words we use as well as the body language of our souls, which reveals our secret intentions. We must allow ourselves to be brought to a place (perhaps finally dashed from the tall tower we were so proudly climbing) where we can hear the quiet God-murmur, "I want to do it in you *myself!*"

We must give up our independence. We must recognize the fact that we are dependent. Waiting on God will become our chief concern. Seeking rest in him will be our primary pastime.

Waiting for God, resting in him, is the hardest form of prayer. It is a wordless communication that reminds us we are not ultimately in control of our lives. There is no thought, no machination, no endeavor that will force God to show his hand. Waiting is the acknowledgment that it is God who has the final word. It is admitting that we cannot do it by ourselves.

It is a practice excercised over the daily living of our lives. When we take long years to become proficient in the playing of a concerto, we must not become discouraged, but remind ourselves that all beginners start with the C-scales. One day we will take our position in the orchestra pit; we will be playing in the concert, but that will require much dedicated work.

When I began to experience the deeper spiritual life, I became hungry for the Word of God. I started to pore over the Scriptures for hours. I discovered verse after verse that dealt with this principle.

"In returning and rest you shall be saved; in quietness and in trust shall be your strength," writes Isaiah (30:15).

The same prophet reiterates this message in 40: 31: ". . . but they who wait for the Lord shall renew their strength, they shall mount up with wings like eagles, they shall run and not be weary, they shall walk and not faint."

Christ's discourse on the vine and the branches in John 15 is basically a sermon on this chapter's topic. "I am the vine, you are the branches. He who abides in me, and I in him, he it is that bears much fruit, for apart from me you can do nothing" (v. 5). The Lord seems to hold an opinion that contradicts the old cry, "I can do it by myself!"

Hebrews develops a difficult-to-understand exposition on the rest that God gives to those who are not rebellious like those children of Israel, stamping their feet in the wilderness. "So then, there remains a sabbath rest for the people of God; for whoever enters God's rest also ceases from his labors as God did from his. Let us therefore strive to enter that rest, that no one fall by the same sort of disobedience" (Heb. 4: 9-11).

What a message to our humanistic, self-oriented, do-it-yourself society! What a word of caution to a church aping its culture. "Be still and cease in your striving" (your praying hard, working long, refusing, struggling, clenching, and hanging on *without God* efforts). "Stop the time-consuming activity. Put aside everything you have substituted for me. Wait, wait, I am coming to your side with my own building plans. Rest, rest. Sabbath in me. I will do the work in you."

The supernatural ability of God to intervene in our human condition is one of the most important teachings of Scripture that we can understand. We must regain the view of a sacramental God.

When I use the word *sacrament*, I am not employing it in reference to the traditional sacraments of the liturgical churches. There are many in "sacramental" churches who have lost their sacramental understanding of God. I am employing it in its general sense, defining a sacrament as anything through which God chooses to infuse his grace. This may be any means whatsoever.

This understanding is important because there is no doctrine of spiritual importance that does not depend upon this supernatural intervention. Redemption, reconciliation, justification, salvation, forgiveness—these are a few of the hundreds of word symbols dealing with something that God does for us in time and space.

True, there is human responsibility. I do not deny it. We are caretakers of the tip of the iceberg of the mind, our wills. They must be brought to a point of obedience. We must reach out to receive. We must turn the offered key. But it is always a response to the initiative of God. He knocks. He comes to show us how to live. He enters. He demonstrates forgiveness.

Sometimes I think we do nothing all our lives but respond to him. The simple truth is: We rarely can do it on our own.

This often is the reason forgiveness doesn't "take," why we don't feel any release from our guilt. We are held back because we have slipped the world's philosophies into the opening of our hearts' doors. Without proper keys, we have forced entry. We drag out unseemly things in disorderly fashion to parade before prying eyes—there is no healing in this. We do all the human things. We carefully examine the doctrine of forgiveness. We have heard it preached from our pulpits, so we know all the right words to say. But symbiosis has not occurred. *We have forgotten to wait for God. We have neglected to wait for his Sabbath in us.*

Simply, we have run ahead on our own. God is far out of our sight. We have said the words of forgiveness, but we don't know enough to wait for the supernatural work of forgiveness in our lives.

When the supernatural has joined us, when symbiosis has occurred, we will know it. It will be recognizable. Our responsibility for forgiveness is to be *obedient*, to utter the appropriate phrases, "Forgive me! I forgive!" Then we must recognize that we are dependent. We cannot do it ourselves. We must wait for the Master Architect who designs all interior structures. We must rest while he does his work in us.

God is the One who constructs Canterburys within. The tidy housekeeper is a tradeswoman under his hire. We are simply apprentices in this fine art.

Relax, rest in the confidence that he knows what he is about. The blueprints are in his hands. Don't leave until he has finished his task. Sit yourself down under the vine shade. Let it tendril and curl about you until it becomes rooted in your being, entwined around your soul, until symbiosis has been achieved.

He is the One who knows all there is to know about tower building. He creates homes within. He becomes home for us.

None other Lamb, none other Name,
None other hope in heaven or earth or sea,
None other hiding-place from guilt and shame,
    None beside Thee.

My faith burns low, my hope burns low;
Only my heart's desire cries out in me
By the deep thunder of its want and woe,
    Cries out to Thee.

Lord, Thou art life, though I be dead;
Love's fire Thou art, however cold I be;

Nor heaven have I, nor place to lay my head,
Nor home, but Thee.

Christina Rossetti

LIFE RESPONSE

Is there any Babel tower-building going on in your life?
Examine yourself and see if you can discover any
undue spiritual independence. No? Well, take your
courage in hand and ask a close friend to help you identify
any of the ways you may be crying, "I can do it by
myself!" Uproot any evidence that you may be shaking
your fist in the face of God. Take even more courage in
hand and dare to breathe the prayer, "Dear Master
Builder, if there is any hidden human arrogance in me, I
give you permission to make it plain to me in the days
ahead."

Then memorize portions from John 15. "I am the true
vine, and my Father is the vinedresser. . . . Abide in me,
and I in you." Watch for a fresh knowledge of God, a
knowing of experience. Spiritual symbiosis is always
hastened by Scripture memorization and meditation.

Give me hunger,
O you gods that sit and give
The world its orders.
Give me hunger, pain and want,
Shut me out with shame and failure
From your doors of gold and fame,
Give me your shabbiest, weariest hunger!

But leave me a little love,
A voice to speak to me in the day end,
A hand to touch me in the dark room
Breaking the long loneliness.
In the dusk of the day-shapes
Blurring the sunset,
One little wandering, western star
Thrust out from the changing shores of shadow.
Let me go to the window,
Watch there the day-shapes of dusk
And wait and know the coming
Of a little love.

"AT A WINDOW"
Carl Sandburg

EIGHT
The Mobile Love Unit

A friend had been sharing some tales of woe regarding her in-laws. Finally she cried, "I'll never be able to forgive them! They've done too much to hurt us!"

At one time or another we've all felt that way. A friend, a parent, a child, or an acquaintance has injured us too deeply to "merit" forgiveness. Yet this is exactly the point—"to err is human, to forgive divine." There are circumstances in which it is impossible for us to forgive. We are dependent upon supernatural intervention. God must come and do the work within.

The results of forgiveness are well worth the struggle of yanking our wills to the painful point of obedience. Finding the possible in the impossible is always a thrill. It jolts our stodgy humanity.

For many of us, the results of forgiveness are instantaneous. In my own experience, because I had not suffered the cumulative effects of massive interior boarding, and because I was only in my late twenties, there were immediate happy consequences. For others, a longer process of reconstruction may be necessary. The healing of the past may take several years. Yet even a few years, in comparison to a lifetime, is relatively short.

One of the immediate results of forgiveness we will all experience is an emotional release. Something begins to creak open in our souls. The guilt vanishes; the pain disintegrates. There is an interior letting go of something ugly we had been clutching tightly. It is as though our spirit takes a deep soulish sigh—*"ah-h-h-h-h-h."* The chains that once bound us to another person in hate simply drop away. The river of bitterness against which we have stacked sandbags suddenly ceases surging in her channels and is no longer an emotional threat. What's more, mysteriously, the person we once refused to forgive also experiences a release—without our saying a word to him.

"The sins you retain shall be retained . . ." spoke Christ to his disciples in the upper room. "Whatever you bind on earth shall be bound in heaven," was the authority he vested in those who were members of his church.

"I so profited from your session on forgiveness," one man wrote to me. "It was painful, but rewarding! I realized I had never forgiven my grandfather for abusing me. I was raised in his home after my own father died; my grandfather was an alcoholic for years. Even after he was able to quit drinking, he was an atheist. I was saved as a small child, and I've been praying for his salvation most of my life.

"My grandmother died last year, praising the Lord after months of the torture of cancer. She never lost faith!

Her death only seemed to harden my grandfather all the more. He couldn't understand a God who would allow this suffering.

"After I came home from your session, my heart completely cleansed, I noticed a change in my grandfather. When I mentioned the Lord, he didn't curse. He really seemed to have mellowed! When I talked about him going to church with us, he didn't say no.

"You see, this is really a miracle. My wife and children can even see a difference in grandpa! He has *never* been to a church service!"

In psychological terms, the grandparent changed because the grandson changed; but I have seen this case study duplicated numbers of times, often when there is a geographical separation of thousands of miles and *no* personal contact. A young person on drugs, living far across the country, is forgiven by his parent for the agony he has caused. Suddenly the child telephones his parent for the first time in years and begins making a way back to God, a modern prodigal returning home. These instances make me suspect that something more than the natural is at work here.

When we refuse to forgive one who has wounded us, we are bound together in a duel armlock. In some way, this binding prevents us from receiving God's love, but it also hinders that same love from pouring into the heart of the one who caused us pain. Is this not a bondage of magnificent proportions? When I refuse to forgive a husband, a friend, am I blocking that person from turning to the very God I am praying he will find?

Of course, people sense when they have been forgiven. There is something new and fresh about a relationship once gone stale. The letters begin to wing homeward. A phone call comes after months of quiet. There is warmth in a voice that once was cool.

It only follows that if bitterness disappears on the part of one individual—if there is no mortar to hold together the stone wall—it will crumble. In a tug-of-war, when one team ceases to strain and struggle, when one end of the rope is dropped, the contest is over. So it is with our human tensions.

Yet there is something more at work than just human reactions to human adjustments. It is as though we are bound together with millions of invisible cords, in a corporate ball of twine. When you sin against me, I turn away from you, tightening the strand between us. When I sin against you, you do the same. A pulling against one another occurs, a chafing, a tautness. Our lives, in effect, are in uncomfortable traction.

If we pull against one another when we give pain, do we wind and wind ourselves within these joining fibers until we become cocoonlike toward one another and toward God, struggling in the mummy wrappings of our souls?

I don't know. I only know that when we refuse to forgive, we are bound, and the one whose pain we are unwilling to bear is bound as well. Forgiveness provides release from the spider's web. It is the mother's fingers straightening out the shoelace knots. We experience emotional and psychological release.

Another result of forgiveness that makes difficult forgiving worthwhile is cessation of pain of the past. "We will know we have forgiven," writes Agnes Sanford, "when we can look back on what used to cause us pain with joy." Now that is amazing, but then it is an amazing work of God, forgiveness. (Doesn't the memory of torturous Calvary now gladden the heart of Christ?)

I suppose our soul sings because when we have hauled up our obedience, in the very midst of pain, there is a sudden symbiosis with God. Saint Augustine wrote the words, "Our hearts are ever restless till they find their rest in Thee." In supernatural forgiveness, forgiveness for the impossible, we find our rest in him. He turns the sorrowing into joy. The barren hills, the wastelands in our spirits are made fertile. He turns the brackish waters into sweet.

Have you ever wished you could have seen the leper's skin, rotting and scabbed and ulcerated, grow suddenly pink or brown again under the touch of Christ? I would love to have seen that. What a wonder to have watched the legions of demons flee the Gadarene, insanity spinning from the wild, wide eyes, reason sitting down upon its owner's head.

Have you ever wished you could have viewed Lazarus waddling from the tomb, his body gravecloth-bound? Have you ever grieved at death and longed to be the Nain widow watching Christ's hand clutch the bier, seeing him grasp the cold fingers? Oh, how we long to see earthly bonds vanquished, to see the invasion of the supernatural into our material world!

This is exactly what happens when forgiveness occurs. This is the source of our joy. We are forgiven for the unthinkable. We in turn forgive the impossible. Spiritual symbiosis takes place.

Here comes the phoenix springing from the gray ashes of yesterday. The doors to our hearts have been unlocked, but more—God has been here. He has walked into the rooms. See the imprint where his hand rested upon the mantel! We can eat oatmeal when we've never been able to eat it before. We can laugh when only dry choking was once familiar. Some of us learn to cry and others cease. His feet have paced these floors. The odor of his presence lingers in the air. We are becoming hallowed within.

I had the privilege of hearing Maria Zietner Linke, the

co-author of *East Wind*, talk about her experience after the Second World War. A German citizen, she was taken captive by Russian soldiers in the confusion of the partitioning of Germany at the conflict's end. For three days she was at the mercy of drunken men. "The spoils of war were in this truck. To the victors belonged the toasters, the typewriters, the coffeepots—and my defenseless body." She was repeatedly violated.

At the end of these hellish days, the soldiers stopped the truck in which they were transporting their "spoils," and in an alcoholic stupor, threw one end of a rope around the branch of an apple tree. The other end was tightened around Maria's neck. *Maria*, said a voice in her heart. *You have never witnessed of my love for you.* (Really, the moments in which this supernatural voice communicates, and the messages He conveys are amazing!)

In the auditorium where I was listening, Maria told how, with a twisted length of rope around her neck, she looked at her captors, her tormentors, and asked, "I know where I will go if you kill me. I will go into the arms of Jesus. But where will you go when you die?"

Loud laughter was the only response. She was yanked to her feet. Soon she felt the rough hemp against her neck, but she was no longer afraid.

"Father, forgive them . . ." she heard herself say. Then everything—soldiers, apple blossoms, rope—disappeared into merciful unconsciousness.

When she awoke she was again in the van, an army coat covering her naked body. A detachment of German soldiers had suddenly appeared, shooting their guns and killing the Russian captain. Maria says, "I like to think that my Father had sent his angels to protect me."

This terrible story was shared with such obvious peace, and even with humor, that when I later conducted my assigned workshop, a session on the work of forgiveness, many women who had experienced similar awful assaults (some never having breathed their agony to anyone, not friends, not husband) felt the healing hand of God.

Forgiveness frees us from the past, and because of the interaction of the Lord in our moment of pain—at that point when he takes our disease, our guilt, our distress onto himself—we have joy in the looking back. The redemption of our past also enables us to be channels of healing to those dwelling in broken shanties in their own souls.

"Father, forgive them. . . ." What a cry! The more we say these painful words, the quicker the results of forgiveness come. We become practitioners in a difficult but satisfying art.

The last thing forgiveness does for us is free us to love. We learn to care for our neighbors as ourselves. We begin to learn the meaning of an open, loving heart.

The heart is like a mobile love unit. We take it with us into this world wherever we go. It's no use to God if it is boarded shut; but unboarded, the heart has an immense capacity to embrace.

After years of work, I am beginning to experience the meaning of an open heart. Hospitality, inviting people into my home, has always come easily for me, although I have had much to learn about it. But the hospitality of the open heart, inviting people into the rooms of my soul— that has been harder. I have a natural reserve that many find slightly forbidding. Just recently, however, I've been practicing the prayer, "Lord, this person, this stranger, this friend whose faults have become familiar, is your child. Help me to be a vehicle of your love to this one you have made and cherish."

I have come to the conclusion that it is not enough to attempt to give human love. Human love is not enough.

It too often manipulates or gets entangled with egoistic needs. It tries to impress. It serves for service in return. These days, I don't even struggle to love people. My efforts are concentrated on being open to God—windows wide, double-bolts unlocked, fires burning on the hearth—so that his footmarks and fingerprints can be seen all over the interior of me. No room for barriers now. I seek forgiveness daily. No blockades here; I forgive as soon as possible.

"Love this creature of yours through me. Help me to be a channel of your love. Let her experience your incarnation within." It is a "practicing" kind of prayer—like playing scales on the piano—, but I am discovering that the mobile love unit works. It's a portable treatment center that specializes in emergencies. It draws people unto itself. Love always calls forth love.

On a trip out East, I knew I had been awakened two hours earlier in order to be rerouted to fly from Philadelphia instead of Harrisburg. A middle-aged woman grabbed my elbow as we waited to board. "Are you traveling alone?" she inquired, a desperate look in her eyes. She was flying for the first time and was scared to death. She had picked me out in that crowded room, walked to me across the waiting area. I arranged to sit beside her and took time to explain about wheels bumping up and down and the blue skies above storms. I had been rerouted to give emergency comfort.

I knew while flying out of Atlanta why the plane had been full and I was booked into first-class when my seatmate, a doctor, began to tell me about the heartbreak of his recent divorce. I shared with him the healing there is in forgiveness—how important it is to come into contact with the supernatural, how God is the source of all wholeness in my life. The sympathetic treatment center was in operation.

I knew why I was traveling from Omaha to Chicago when a young mother struggled to the ticket counter in front of me, juggling an infant, a two year old, a German shepherd, a diaper bag, a coat, and a flight case. I had intended to pray during this flight, longing for quiet, but James kept whispering over my shoulder something about faith without works being dead. I sat in the smoking section (I don't smoke!) and cradled the infant, then steered my new friend through O'Hare as she caught her next flight to meet her husband, a Navy man who had been transferred. I had been booked on this plane to provide traveler's aid.

People I've never met tell me about their agony, their pains, their life disasters. Whenever I can, I tell them about God. Simply, my heart is becoming an emergency first-aid base, a tool of redemption in this dying world. A prayer is being answered. He is pouring his love into me.

A verification of this came from an unlikely source recently—from one of the airport drivers who sometimes picks me up as I travel between home and O'Hare. We had been talking about our work and I mentioned that I wrote about things in which I believed, that there was enough hopelessness in this world, and I felt that people ought to hear that there was an option: that they could experience goodness through an encounter with Jesus Christ.

"You know," he said, "we were talking about you down in the limousine pool the other day."

I readied myself for whatever blow might be coming. I could just imagine what the drivers might have to say about me.

"I think you should keep on writing and speaking. Goodness comes from you."

Goodness comes from me—from me? It is *God*ness, his love being poured into the once-desolate places.

Help me, Lord, help me never to forget that eyes may be watching. Don't allow me for a moment to slam closed any doors you want opened. Keep me learning the meaning of an open heart.

We forgive. We yank our wills to obedience. We acquiesce to bearing the pain and then find that he has taken our distresses upon himself. We experience release, the person we have hated is unbound. There is joy in the looking back. We become able to love. Nothing is impossible with God.

LIFE RESPONSE

What is the condition of your open heart? Has it become a mobile love unit yet?

Practice the prayer, "Lord, fill me with your love for this your child." Try to remember to pray it with each human contact of your day. Here is a child. Breathe the prayer. Here is a roommate. Implore God's love before saying a word. Here is a spouse. A little love, Lord. Here is a colleague. . . .

Check your progress each night. Examine all the relationships that have occurred each day. Ask youself, "Did I remember to pray? Did I experience God's love flowing through me?"

Remember that this kind of loving takes some practice. Don't be discouraged if you fumble over the first scales. Proficiency won't be far behind.

His heart, to me, was a place of palaces and pinnacles
and shining towers;
I saw it then as we see things in dreams,—I do not
remember how long I slept;
I remember the trees, and the high, white walls, and how
the sun was always on the towers;
The walls are standing today, and the gates: I have been
through the gates, I have groped, I have crept
Back, back. There is dust in the streets, and blood; they
are empty; darkness is over them;
His heart is a place with the lights gone out, forsaken by
great winds and the heavenly rain, unclean and
unswept,
Like the heart of the holy city, old, blind, beautiful
Jerusalem,
Over which Christ wept.

"I HAVE BEEN THROUGH THE GATES"
Charlotte Mew

NINE
Junk-away Day

One of my little boys recently brought home an aluminum jello mold, which he had proudly salvaged from a neighbor's refuse pile. When I responded less than enthusiastically, my daughter reminded me, "Mother, you used to go garbage-picking yourself."

How true. Sometimes it seems that practically everything in our home has been salvaged from someone's garbage pile!

I am the official hand-me-down depot for our entire family. My sister bemoans the fact that she is in Florida while I am here in Illinois, close to the attic in the family farm and the interesting artifacts in our parents' basement. (We have a family understanding: If it's in the garage or the basement, it's for the taking.) Unfortunately, she feels that I always get there before her.

In the township where we used to live, there was a community activity we celebrated called Junk-away Day. All the residents were invited to place anything they wished to discard in the alleys: refrigerators, broken-down washing machines, unappreciated pieces of furniture. All the flotsam and jetsam of living could be piled to await special garbage details that were assigned to remove it.

"Junk-away Day is tomorrow," my neighbors would say, an eager gleam in their eyes. We particularly anticipated the Saturday pickup assigned to the north end of our town. Here posh homes, many of them refurbished samples of "prairie architecture," dotted the wide lawns. It was an opportunity to take a car and roam up and down the alleys in the hopes of spotting a find.

The children were especially delighted with this community treasure hunt. "You remember," my daughter reminded me, "when I found that little old stove, and you painted it black and put it on the front porch with geraniums in it?"

I'll admit it—I often profited from Junk-away Day. Finally, however, I was forced by the accumulating clutter to establish a firm rule. Junk-away Day was for getting *rid* of things; it was not for discarding our old hoards and then gaining new rubbish.

The same principle should be followed in our souls. After forgiveness has occurred, a junk-away day begins in our hearts. Here is a closet full of anger, a vestibule hiding umbrella prongs of pain. It is time for a spring cleaning. May has come again. Drag out all the old clutter. Be wise enough not to replace the old garbage with the new. (What joy we will be bringing to the tidy housekeeper!)

116

Every few years the newspapers report the death of an eccentric, living in utter squalor but with a sizable reserve of funds stashed away in some bank. The riddle of such a person's existence was fictionalized several years ago in a book entitled *My Brother's Keeper.* In it, two old men, brothers, are found dead in a house crammed from cellar to roof with one hundred- and seventy tons of hoarded rubbish.

These men of good family, from a cultivated background, had become recluses in the familial mansion, located in a now-crumbling neighborhood in town. The old house was stacked to the eaves with a puzzling agglomeration of useless objects: old pianos, fourteen of them, the chassis of a vintage automobile in the cellar, mountains of pickings from old junkyards. Bundled newspapers were piled into the rooms to make them solid cubes, pierced only by a cunning system of tunnels that were threaded with death-dealing booby traps. Under one of the traps the body of one brother was found. The second brother was discovered nearby, dead of starvation.

Why? This, of course, is the question the book seeks to answer. And "Why?" is the question to ask concerning our own souls. How did we become so full of garbage, and how can the accumulated junk be discarded before it becomes our own death trap?

We must force ourselves to understand that after the key of forgiveness has opened the locked doors of our hearts, there is always a cleaning-up process that must occur.

A rebuilding must take place after the disasters of sin. The twine-bound hoards of yesterday's newspapers will have to be discarded. A fumigation of the pests that gnaw on our spirits will have to be undertaken. The holes in our battered emotional drywall will need to be replastered. Broken fences will need mending.

If we lose sight of the fact that God is the Master Builder of our souls, we are headed, now as much as ever, for trouble. It is most important to continue waiting on his reading of the blueprints, his plans for making the interior rooms functional again. There are booby traps in this junk-away process that his wisdom can keep us from springing.

Among the first items we are going to have to haul away are the haunting sounds of past painful memories, particularly after God has done the supernatural work of forgiveness in our hearts. Corrie ten Boom calls these the "ding-dongs." She illustrates this by reminding us of the bell in a bell tower. After the bell ringer is done pulling the rope, the clapper still swings for a little while, causing a few remnant clatters.

When God has touched our lives, removing guilt or pain, often there are a few haunting clamors, some left-over discordant peels. Miss ten Boom recommends that we not be abashed by these jangling reminders, but gently remind ourselves that "those are simply the ding-dongs." There is no reason to be frightened or to even give them much attention.

We will not allow ourselves to be thrown by this favorite tool of our enemy, the casting of doubts on God's touch. We will not allow him to shred our fragile-winged hope with these reminders of our pain and guilt from the past. God is seeking to ring a new song in our souls, and we will do well to refuse the ding-dongs, resting confidently in whatever spiritual symbiosis we know we have achieved. In the middle of the mess of housecleaning, it is wise to remind ourselves of the fingerprints of God we discovered before we undertook our exasperating tasks. Surely some progress has been made.

Often, after we have received God's forgiveness, we

are prone to fill the household with guilt when we wander into the same sins again. We are in danger of repeating the debilitation. A bully is threatening to inhabit our hearts, the bully of our own flaw. Quickly we must confess and receive godly absolution before a door is pushed shut.

Three street rules have helped me in previous gang wars, when my territory has been threatened with invasion. One: In order to gain the upper hand over a browbeating flaw, I must be willing to commit myself to bloody battle. In other words, this fight-to-the-finish struggle will become a priority item in my life. Two: A realistic time limit must be set in order to strategically plot my victory. Three: It is absolutely imperative that I remember I have a Defender on whom I can call.

The bully I'm fighting against right now is overweight. I need to shed ten extra pounds that I have carried over the last several years. How defeated I feel each evening when I realize I've failed again that day. How often I've confessed and asked for absolution. (God has certainly gone over the 490 forgiveness quota with me!)

Sitting myself down and designing an efficient weight-loss system is demanding. It means I will have to establish an exercise program that will take into account my hatred of calisthenics. I may have to research various approaches to physical fitness. A reasonable food-intake philosophy will have to be developed, and this may mean altering the entire family's eating habits (i.e., no junk foods in the house, no empty calories, nothing in the way of tempting and fattening snacks).

To cope, I give close associates (my daughter is especially welcome to exercise her talents) permission to program me verbally. "You'd look great if only you weren't ten pounds overweight! You don't need that fudge sundae. You're making that dress look a little tight."

I decide, after much research, to fast once a week, skip the noon meal, refuse sweets, turn my back on my normal overdoses of good grain breads, jog when the weather permits, find a racquetball partner, do a few tone-up exercises on the living room rug.

"You're really serious about this," some observer might remark. Yes, that's the first rule of street fighting, particularly when a bully is involved. This must become one of the priority items in my life. I am committing myself to a blood and sweat struggle.

The second rule is to establish a realistic time limit. I'm not going to expect to lose ten pounds in a month. My reading tells me that the slower the weight loss, the more likely I will maintain it. Besides, I have to get this flabby body into shape, and it has taken me thirty-five years to get into this predicament. I should be able to notice improvement in six months, and within a year I should be able to reach my goal.

We set ourselves up for defeat when we are not realistic. We will all be disappointed if we think we can create healthy biceps out of underused muscles overnight. Figurative body-building may take some time. There's going to be a lot of pumping iron.

When I have done my share, I must try to remember that I can't do it all. I have a Defender who is ready to come to my side with aid, *but I must remember to call for him*.

Several years ago, I fictionalized one of my husband's sermon illustrations. I think this little story will help to clarify the final street rule.

Rafer was strangling on the dust he'd eaten. With a moan he turned onto his back. Morgan, his great enemy, had waylaid him again on his way home from school.

"Hey, kid! Whatsa madder?" asked a high squeaky

voice. Rafer looked up into the massive frame of a man who leaned over to give him a hand.

"Garciano's my name, Stony Garciano. Don't know me? Well sure, I'se before your time. World Heavyweight Champ-i-on. Only heavy-weight champ-i-on to retire undefeated. Yessir! Never lost a pro bout: forty nine in all, forty three by knockout. Dat big guy jump you much?"

Rafer nodded, still dull from his beating, but awed by this big bull of a man. "Yeah, Morgan's a real mean guy," Rafer agreed. "He gets me every chance he can. Waits in alleys, hallways; I'm scared to go 'round the corner. I try to dodge him, go home different ways, but he always finds me and—"

"Beats da tar outta ya," finished Garciano.

Rafer bowed his head in shame. He felt like a chicken even though Morgan had fifty pounds on him.

Drawing himself to full stature, the boxer flexed the bulging muscles of his back and shoulders, then whispered softly, "There's nuttin' I hate mor'na bully. Tell ya whad I'm gonna do—gonna follow ya everywhere. Stay behind so's nobody can spot me. When dis punk jumps ya again, just give a hollah, and will we ever give dis man Morgan *one big surprise.*" Garciano held up his broad fists, shadow boxed, then winked with a sly grin.

Hope surged through Rafer. Was Morgan ever gonna get his. A battle lust welled in his soul. He felt like tangling with the whole rotten neighborhood.

Rafer began to stalk the streets. The word soon got out that he was looking for Morgan. *Hey, Morgan,* he thought to himself. *Come take your licks.* Garciano always remained a discreet distance behind.

Suddenly, while turning a corner, Rafer found himself face to face with his great enemy. "Hey, kid," menaced Morgan. "Heard ya was lookin' for me."

121

Bravely, Rafer flailed his fists, tripped on his shoelace, and sustained his 268th pummeling from Morgan, the big man of the streets.

Strangling on the dust he'd eaten, Rafer turned around with a moan. He felt someone slapping his cheeks and shouting, "Hey, kid! Hey, kid!"

Rafer focused his eyes. Garciano leaned very close. "Well, kid, ya got it again. Why din'ja call on me?"

Rafer closed his eyes. He didn't want to face the big man who had been trailing him so faithfully. "Why din'ja call?" said a small, quiet voice. "Why in the world din'ja call for help?"

The best place for ruffians is out in the alley where they belong, but we cannot bounce them out without the help of our Defender. We must whistle for help. Or if whistling is contrary to your nature, perhaps you might want to pray the prayer of Amy Carmichael, "Do Thou for me, Lord. Do Thou for me."

I have a feeling that in a year my bully will be under control. He will be out in the alley on his ear.

Often much of the junk in our hearts has accumulated because we have been victims of withheld love. Here lies an assortment of jagged-edged rejections. Here lies a messy pile of poor self-image, the wispy dust balls of bitterness, the moldy sinks of self-pity.

Coming to terms with all this garbage may take years. We may need the professional aid of a good psychological counselor or a patient pastor. But wholeness, cleanliness, whether it takes a year or ten, is possible. That is the hopeful promise to which we all can cling.

There is one practical suggestion I might make in regard to the junking-away of the effects of rejection. A strange paradox exists in regard to loving. Often we begin to learn to love, even when we have had inadequate amounts ourselves, by giving away what little we do have.

In reality, we all have insufficient stores of this commodity. It doesn't really matter how much or how little we have received in the past. It seems as though we are always running short. We must learn to state the fact like the widow in her explanation to Elijah, "There is nothing in the house—except a jar of oil."

After junk-away day has occurred in our souls, often there is not much more left than a pot of oil, a small jar that holds our miserly store of love. The prophet instructed the widow to borrow vessels of all her neighbors and to pour the little that she had from her one pot into all the others until they were full.

God's love is the oil that must be poured into our empty vessel-hearts. Our lives must be swept clean; the bullies sent into waterless places. When God floods the rooms of my subconscious with himself, he pours into my inadequacy from the great storehouse of his adequacy. The more I love, the more rooms I discover. The more I pour away my ointment, the more I increase my capacity to embrace. God is the One who makes me full.

We have all been the victim of withheld love, but we have also been freed by forgiveness to love again. The worst disaster on Junk-away Day in our old town was to forget it had arrived. That meant we had to live with our accumulations crowding our much-needed living space for another year. Let's not miss the opportunities for junk-away days in our souls.

Out with the useless antique attitudes: "But they never do anything for us. The last time we got together, it was at *our* house. How can I possibly write a nice note after the terrible things he said to me? They have hurt us too much to ever act normally toward them again."

No, we are the ones who are free. We must imitate the

123

initiating love of Christ. Our Lord didn't wait for people to do things for him. He didn't sigh in a corner resenting that no one came to talk to him. He wasn't peeved over being ignored in social situations. And he knew all there was to know about rejection.

His was a ministry of initiating love. The verbs that deal with Christ are revealing. He *came;* he *said* to Simon and Andrew, "Follow me"; he *entered* the synagogue and *taught;* he *healed* many who were sick; he *said* to the man who had the withered hand, "Come here"; he *went* up on a mountain and *called* those whom he desired, and he *appointed* twelve; he *said* to the paralytic, "My son, your sins are forgiven."

These were all initiatory actions; none were in response to the inquiry or invitation of others. God's love is the initiating kind. It is first love. "In this is love, not that we loved God but that he loved us and sent his Son to be the expiation for our sins. . . . We love, because he first loved us," writes the apostle John. We must learn to make his love ours.

So we begin the painful process of doing, going, calling, writing, saying, finding, inviting. We choke on our timorous courage but find the strength to pour out our small pots of oil. We breathe the words, "You look so beautiful today. I care deeply about you. I miss you when you aren't here." We tip our tiny vessels in reconciliation.

"Lord, furnish me now with your love for the one I have forgiven. Fill my empty household with your caring so it won't be inhabited by dark and evil beings. Fill me so full of yourself there will be no room for the last state, which is worse than the first. Increase my small pots of oil." This prayer is of utmost importance.

Junk-away day has come to our souls. The musty storage rooms have been unlocked. The time has come to drag out the mice-eaten resentments, the crumpled lampshades of past miseries. Time to haul away the cardboard cartons that once stored our bitter thoughts, the moth-holed upholstery in which we once sat and brooded. There is a new look planned for this household of the soul. Refurbishing is going on. These items are simply not appropriate to the redecorating that is being planned for within.

Haul them away, stack them out in the alley. Empty the cluttered attics. Get rid of the booby death-traps. Whatever you do, don't drag someone else's junk back inside. Mark junk-away day on the calendar so you won't forget. Hang a sign in the window, Roomer Wanted.

You may be surprised at how soon the live-in God of love will answer your advertisement. He is a Lover who longs to inhabit our clean souls.

LIFE RESPONSE

Think about initiating love. Contract with yourself to attempt to give away one act of first-turn love per day. Afraid you'll run out of ideas? You will for sure if you attempt this process outside of prayer. Here is where we find the One who pours love into our meager stores. Here is where we discover surprisingly endless supplies of loving ideas. Here is where we hear directions for the right time, the right place, the right way.

How wonderful that God is never empty. He is always full. He is never "sold-out"!

When you're away, I'm restless, lonely,
Wretched, bored, dejected; only
Here's the rub, my darling dear,
I feel the same when you are near.

"WHEN YOU'RE AWAY"
Samuel Hoffenstein

TEN
Reconstruction:
Lost Loves

A young wife has left her husband of three years; their two-year-old child is in his custody. After several months she returns home only to say, "I'm back, but I don't have any feelings for you."

A married couple comes for counseling. His parents had predicted that the marriage would come to no good. They were totally opposed to this woman with whom their son had fallen in love. Then they set out to do everything within their power to insure that their prophecy would come true. "I'm not divorcing you," the young woman sighs. "I'm divorcing your father."

A little child weeps. "Why are you crying, Eric?"

He responds, "My parents love my brother more than

they love me." It is not just a childhood phobia. Even when grown, he remains convinced that he received only second helpings of his parents' love.

How commonly we suffer lack of love from the people who are supposed to love us most. How frequently we destroy those we should be seeking most to protect. Sadly, this short-circuited loving influences all our living. I wonder if there are any earthly hells more awful than the ones we create in our primary family relationships.

Why do we have such problems loving our relatives?

Sometimes there is simply a conflict of personalities. A child born into one's home is completely incompatible with a parent. One asks the question, "How could my own body have delivered this puzzling, exasperating personality?"

Or perhaps a man is attracted to the strengths in his fiancee's personality. Her eagerness in social situations, her ease in verbalizing enhance his own tight-lipped reserve. After marriage, however, he can see the shadow side of the abilities that once attracted him. She is garrulous, never closing her mouth. She is seldom home, but always off working on community, church, or social projects. He longs for a respite from this pace of life, and some attention.

One reason for our lack of love for our loved ones is that through the years we have come to concentrate on what is bad in one another. The enlarging machine in our minds blows the negative all out of proportion. We have forgotten the gentleness, the delightful sense of the ridiculous, the whimsical outlook on life, the great-heartedness. We can see no good.

Another basic reason for our lack of love is that we have been wronged. A sister-in-law, filled with her own insecurities, is jealous of the love that her own parents now shower on her brother's wife. Her obvious attitude makes family gatherings unpleasant.

The children within a family have grown up encouraged by their parents to compete with each other. Relationships have been forged on the anvil of who could achieve the best grades, who could win in tennis, who collected the most honors on the athletic fields. Now in their adult years, they know no way of relating other than in subtle combat.

A wife has been replaced by her husband's mistress—a woman without a body: his consuming work.

The reasons for not loving those closest to us are inexhaustible. The result, however, is the same. Something has made us close a door in our hearts toward those we should love the most.

Though most of us have reconciled ourselves to living in less than perfectly loving relationships, this state of affairs is tragic. It is tragic because it is not what God, the Creator of families, intended. It is tragic because of its self-perpetuation.

We cannot close our heart to anyone in these primary familial relationships—spouse, brother, child, in-laws—without it affecting, in some way, someone else in our primary familial relationships. There is an uncanny cause and effect relationship that often sets off a chain of rejections within the family unit. A closed door of any kind is a barrier against love.

For instance, perhaps I have grown to harbor subtle hatred toward one of my parents. It is not overt. I do not go around saying, "I hate my father, my mother," but the despicable emotion is there just the same.

There have been understandable causes for this plank nailed across the door jambs. One person was beaten as a child. One's mother was wanton sexually and dragged through the house all the liaisons of her life. One woman

131

was sexually abused by her own father. A heart must be closed against these perversions.

Unfortunately, that closed door prevents us from loving someone else in the primary family relationship. The abused child is often the adult who abuses his or her own child.

A daughter reminds her father of his own mother. She's not loose, just a flirt, but in his subconscious he is terrified. He has been on guard against this type of thing all his life. He clamps down on the teen, accusing her of things about which she had never dreamed. The confidence between them is shattered.

A woman's concept of sexuality has been so damaged by encounters in her father's bed that she is frigid in her own marriage bed.

Often the damage we sustain has not been so extreme. It is not as hideous as the results of child abuse or incest. The implications, nevertheless, are often similar. They incline us toward malfunctioning in the giving of love to our own close ones.

Perhaps a parent has never been able to say anything positive to us. Day in and day out our fragile self-esteem has been shredded by this constant negativism. We determine that we will not be the same way with our own families, but although we say the words, our praise often tumbles out in the wrong ways or for the wrong things. We cannot be natural when we are so on guard against the past. Our own insecurities trip up our good intentions.

Or an in-law always acts testy, making us dread family gatherings. We become emotional about that relative whenever he or she begins to draw near. Christmas, Thanksgiving, Memorial Day—all the traditional times for family celebrations become potential battlegrounds in our own home. Our spouse doesn't understand our crankiness, our crying jags. He was "born and bred in the briar patch," to quote Br'er Rabbit in the "Uncle Remus" tales. Consequently, he has learned to cope with the thorns. Our attitude forces him to choose between us and his family. We reject our in-laws, but at the same time we are also rejecting a part of our spouse.

Perhaps we see a grandparent favoring our sister's child. This is unsettling to us personally, but all the more so because we are aware that our own children are intuitive about this preference. We watch as our children close themselves off, pretending in their small hearts that they don't care anyway. They say they would rather be with their own friends, and we grieve that they are losing the delightful memories that can be associated with cousins. It is amazing that even at early ages, the cycle of closed doors begins to have its effect.

Isn't it wonderful to know that the Lord has come to redeem us from this endless merry-go-round of disappointments? Forgiveness, of course, is the place where we begin to restore our lost love for our relatives.

Forgiveness, however, is extremely difficult among these primary ties, because we are dealing with all the core memories, the root causes of most of our subliminal motivations and drives. It is a laborious task and needs to be undertaken with a willingness to repeatedly forgive (after every holiday celebration, for instance, or after every dinner hour!). We must determinedly vow, "I will forgive all past sins; I will forgive whenever I remember old wounds or when I receive fresh ones."

There is a chilling plea recorded in Arthur Miller's play, *The Crucible*, set in Salem, Massachusetts, during the witch trials of the 1700s. John Proctor, the anti-hero of this story, has been discovered by his wife, Elizabeth, in a compromising intimacy with a younger hired woman. He confesses. The girl is sent away. Now the

133

couple must live out their disaster.

"Spare me!" Proctor pleads. "You forget nothin' and forgive nothin'. Learn charity, woman. I have gone tiptoe in this house all seven months since she is gone. I have not moved from here to there without I think to please you, and still an everlasting funeral marches round your heart. I cannot speak but what I am doubted, every moment judged for lies, as though I come into a court when I come into this house!"

Forgiveness silences the funeral dirges. It puts away the black crepe, dismantles the mourning wreaths, stores the arm bands. Without it, we are forced to grieve continually in the cemeteries of our dead hopes. We must say, "I am willing to bear the pain."

The results of forgiveness are well worth our painful willingness. The innocent recipient of our blocked love is restored to his rightful position in our hearts. In essence, we forgive a mother for the sake of our own child. We forgive an uncle his homosexuality for the sake of being able to love the son who resembles him. We stoke the flames of our inward heart with the fresh fuel of forgiveness in order to ward against the cold dampness that seeks to creep in at the windows, the doors.

Then we junk-away. We get rid of the old resentments. We confess our hatreds, our jealousies, our raging competitiveness. We promise never again to deliberately board our hearts.

When the household has been cleansed and swept, we look at the meager, half-empty pot and pray for God's love to now fill us for these, our loved ones. We are dependent upon him pouring himself into our washed vessels.

When it comes to loving our own families, it is again important to remember that human love is never enough. How terrified we become when we realize we no longer feel any love for a spouse. How terrible for a parent to have to come to terms with the fact that he has never loved a certain child the way that child needed to be loved.

Human love is a well that runs dry. It empties during the famine of another's emotional deprivation. It becomes bitter when poisons from another's attitude continually seep in. How amazed we are when we discover that bloodlines do not insure loving relationships! We will be much better off if we accept the more realistic picture that we will never have enough love; if we come to terms with the fact that we will have to pray repeatedly, "Lord, give me *your* love for this my father, my child, my wife, my in-law."

We must come to realize that we need another source, a wellspring that can supply our deficient flows of living water. That wellspring, of course, is the love of God. Only then will there be love enough.

The process of rebuilding lost love for those in our own family units is long and arduous. First of all, we must be willing to tip our pots and pour out what little we have into the lives of those around us.

We begin to take the infant-steps of initiating love. We call that cantankerous father-in-law and ask how his day is going. We write a note that reminds a sister of what good times we used to share. We conscientiously begin to restructure our pattern of relating to a child under our own roof. Slowly, cautiously, patiently—the progress is tedious, but one day we may discover that love draws love unto itself.

One of the mental exercises that will help us in the giving away of God's love is to begin to concentrate on what is good in a personality instead of focusing on what is bad. Admittedly, this is going to be hard for some of us.

A game we play in our family is called the "What's Bad About, What's Good About Game." The whole gang is gathered. It is time for a clearing of the air of our living together. "What's bad about so-and-so?" we begin. (Everyone gets his turn, parents included.) "What do you think this one needs to learn to do better?" Generally, everyone has some little gripe he wants to get off his chest. "Joel teases too much." "Mother doesn't listen when we talk to her." "Daddy's been too busy."

In the warm circle of our trusting family, this is a surprisingly nonthreatening exercise, witnessed to by the eagerly raised hands of the little ones. "My turn next! Do me now! Me! Me!" Perhaps our trust is enhanced because we do not belabor our weak areas, but rather pledge ourselves to support one another in the overcoming of the flaw. "How about if we pray with you each night, Joel, and ask God to take Mr. Teasing out of your heart? Maybe you don't feel mommy and daddy give you enough attention, and this is the way you tell us about it. What special things would you like to do just with us?"

The children devised signals to capture my attention after we discussed the fact that I was often unapproachable. Now the youngest child chimes a little couplet, "Mother dear, may I have your ear?" I had become immune to his persistent tap-tap-tapping on my shoulder, but I never seem to fail to hear the sing-song.

One of the teens worked out her own system. She cries, "Earth calling mother. Earth calling mother. Are you there, mother? Come in, mother. Come in."

After the negative has been handled, we turn our attention toward discovering what is good. We always end our sessions with the positive. "What do we like about one another?" Admittedly, facility in this second area was a little slower in the coming, but proficiency was not really far behind.

What wonderful things we discovered in telling what we most valued in each other. "Joel teases me sometimes, but he really is my best friend."

"I'm so glad I have parents like you. I'd hate to have the parents some other kids have."

If you have been bogged down in the miry quicksand of criticism, take a moment to discover what is good, then communicate it. Perhaps your search will be aided by the prayer, "Father, help me to see these my loved ones through your eyes."

The revelation of God's viewpoint helps me in my loving. Often I can then understand why one acts the way he does, why one neglects our relationship, why one is not interested in the things I am doing. Mostly, however, this prayer gives me glimpses of the good, a sudden flash of beauty I had forgotten, the marvelous potential that God is cultivating.

Then work at your loving. Make it initiatory. Take a trip to the library, collect several anthologies of love poetry, bring them home and copy a few of your favorites to leave as grace notes in the lunches, on the pillows, in the notebooks, or in the mail of any of the loved ones you are attempting to love better.

Recently, I heard about a woman from a broken family background who had also experienced a divorce with a resultant separation from her own children. She established a precedent of writing to her children on their birthdays and sharing with them a special memory from her own past. This was to insure a continuity in the generations as well as to develop a better knowledge of herself. Then she wrote to her parents as well, telling them each year of a happy memory they had provided when she had been a child in their home. "I don't want them to grow old thinking they did everything wrong," she explains.

Establish family traditions that will enhance your love relationships. My mother-in-law used to explain, "We must *make* our own happy memories." The power of this is in our own hands. The requirement that renders any activity a tradition is that upon looking back we will find ourselves musing. "Mary and I *always* . . . The men in our family *always* . . . Mother *always* . . ." These statements must be followed by a warm-bunting feeling, a wraparound kind of blanket security, a sit-by-the-fireplace glow. Traditions are like the cup of water that primes the old kitchen pump. Love soon comes gushing.

Go hunting for wild watercress in the spring when the snows are barely off the clear country brooks—go with your mother-in-law who is wild about watercress. Each year, treat your sister-in-law to a celebration breakfast on the day in fall when the kids all go back to school. Take a yearly vacation jaunt with your mother who is now widowed. Set aside one night a month to read poetry, out loud, with your husband.

Christ's love is the initiatory kind of love. We must work creatively to find ways to express that kind of caring to those people with whom we are supposed to be in love.

Another love aid that I have established is the regular habit of praying for our family members before I fall to sleep each night. It is an activity that insures loving feelings. I remember their little crises as well as their large ones. I concentrate on their personality development, their spiritual, emotional, physical, and social growth. I talk to the Lord about my attitudes toward them.

Regularly, he gives me a tender heart. I love my husband more each night when I fall asleep than I have loved him that day. I am reminded of the special beauties of each of these my family members. I know something more of the commendation in Ephesians—why husbands were told to love their wives as Christ loved the church. There must be something sacramental in all our extended relationships, something of God, lest they fail. My evening prayers are the time when I implore God to be with me in my loving.

GRANT ME THE KIND OF LOVE

that does not keep old scores.
    Let me be unfettered
    from old tallies
    from old whiplashes
    from old borrowing and not returning.
Let me forget all these.
The straw-stuffed scarecrow
kind of love with coat and hat
retrieved from old trunks—
let me own none of these.
    Let me know every morning new-day
    kind of love: dew-wet, garden-fresh,
    growing kind of love
a not-afraid-of-being-hurt,
or wounded kind of love—
a love that does not syncopate,
or change the meaning of the word.
A love that does not shun toll roads—
nor yet mind byroads
    and never counts the cost.

                        Wilma Burton

LIFE RESPONSE

Name one person in your family you have trouble

loving. Think about a tradition you can start that will bring this individual pleasure. Pray about it. Let God give you his viewpoint about this loved one, an idea that will prime the pump of your love. What could you do that would bring pleasure to this difficult personality?

Do it.

Love divine, all loves excelling,
Joy of heaven, to earth come down;
Fix in us Thy humble dwelling;
All Thy faithful mercies crown.
Jesus, Thou art all compassion,
Pure, unbounded love Thou art;
Visit us with Thy salvation;
Enter every trembling heart.

Breathe, O breathe Thy loving Spirit
Into every troubled breast!
Let us all in Thee inherit,
Let us find that second rest.
Take away our bent to sinning,
Alpha and Omega be;
End of faith, as its beginning,
Set our hearts at liberty.

Come, almighty to deliver,
Let us all Thy life receive;
Suddenly return, and never,
Nevermore Thy temples leave:
Thee we would be always blessing,
Serve Thee as Thy hosts above,
Pray, and praise Thee without ceasing,
Glory in Thy perfect love.

Finish then Thy new creation,
Pure and spotless let us be;
Let us see Thy great salvation
Perfectly restored in Thee:
Changed from glory into glory,
Till in heaven we take our place,
Till we cast our crowns before Thee,
Lost in wonder, love, and praise.

"LOVE DIVINE"
Charles Wesley

ELEVEN
A Brawling Bride in the Household of God?

The wedding guests have gathered in great anticipation; the ceremony to be performed today has been long awaited. The orchestra begins to play an anthem, and the choir rises in proper precision. The bridegroom and his attendants gather in front of the chancel. One little saint, her flowered hat bobbing, leans to her companion and whispers, "Isn't he handsome?" The response is agreement, "My, yes. The handsomest."

One by one, the bridesmaids, heralds of the nuptials, begin to stride in measured patterns. Several flower girls sow rose petals upon the white, unmarked aisle cloth. The sound of the organ rises, a joyous announcement that the bride is coming. Everyone stands and strains to get a proper glimpse of the beauty—then a horrible gasp explodes from the congregation. This is a bride like no other.

In she stumbles—something terrible has happened! One leg is twisted; she limps pronouncedly. The wedding garment is tattered and muddy; great rents in the dress leave her scarcely modest. Black bruises can be seen welting her bare arms; the bride's nose is bloody. An eye is swollen, yellow and purple in its discoloration. Patches of hair look as if they had actually been pulled from her scalp.

Fumbling over the keys, the organist begins again after his shocked pause. The attendants cast their eyes down. The congregation mourns silently. Surely the Bridegroom deserved better than this! That handsome Prince who has kept himself faithful to his love should find consummation with the most beautiful of women—not this. His bride, the church, has been fighting again.

I am a child of the church. My early memories are intertwined with Sunday school teachers, morning worship services, fellowship hours, youth groups, choir practices, evening evangelistic efforts, midweek prayer meetings, summer Bible camps. I was raised in the church, and much of my adult life has been spent serving the church. I am all too aware of church splits, minor fracases, nonamicable partings, ecclesiastical skirmishes.

The church corporate, that household of the living God, has too often formed itself into a series of fortified camps, entrenched not against the enemy without, but against the enemy within. Cold, silent wars or outright major offensives—it doesn't matter which, hostilities are occurring. Word bombardments are being unleashed.

Slaughter is havocking the board meeting. Bloodshed is launched in the women's sewing circle. The bride is brawling again.

Why? Why are so many of our churches filled with this bitterness? Why is it impossible to love those members of our own church families?

"Defending the doctrine!" we respond. "Keeping the faith pure! Protecting the truth against liberalism! Guarding the traditions against parochialism!"

No matter what rationalizations we feebly offer, I think the underlying reason for our warring has been succinctly defined by the apostle James. He writes an exposition that could practically be entitled, "On Brawling Brides":

> What causes wars, and what causes fightings among you? Is it not your passions that are at war in your members? You desire and do not have; so you kill. And you covet and cannot obtain; so you fight and wage war. You do not have, because you do not ask. You ask and do not receive, because you ask wrongly, to spend it on your passions. Unfaithful creatures! (4:1-4a).

The reason for our church disputes is the raging passions of our own hearts. If we really loved one another, we would find the grace to agree to disagree.

("Now, James," I can hear some of us amending, "things are not really so bad. We have never actually killed a church member." We might, at this point, remind ourselves of Christ's discussion on the sixth commandment, "You have heard that it was said to the men of old, 'You shall not kill; and whoever kills shall be liable to judgment.' But I say to you that every one who is angry with his brother shall be liable to judgment; whoever insults his brother shall be liable to the council, and whoever says, 'You fool!' shall be liable to the hell of fire. So if you are offering your gift at the altar, and there remember that your brother has something against you, leave your gift there before the altar and go; first be reconciled to your brother, and then come and offer your gift" (Matt. 5: 22-24).)

Most of the conflicts in churches are over nothing more than matters of opinion. The striving stems from the pitting of my ideas against your ideas. Rarely is there anything inherently moral involved in most of our choices; there is nothing right or wrong, nothing even smacking of doctrine. Even most of our doctrinal disputes, my husband and I have come to conclude, are due to subliminal personality conflicts.

The warring rises from the passions within us. We want the direction of the church to coincide with *our* ideas. We are coveting someone's leadership position. We prove this by refusing to submit. We all secretly desire to be appointed commander in chief (forgetting there is only One who deserves that appointment in the church). We have the audacity to take our own opinion and hang around its neck the clapboard printed God's Will. We are adamant. We deserve James's condemnation. We are, indeed, unfaithful creatures.

It is time to remember that there is a law of love that must be exercised within the Body of Christ. "This is my commandment, that you love one another as I have loved you. Greater love has no man than this, that a man lay down his life for his friends. You are my friends if you do what I command you. . . . This I command you, to love one another" (John 15:12-14, 17).

We are not able to love one another in the Body of Christ because we are suffering from the disasters of sin. We are helpless in the face of our old dilemma. We are in need of a reconstruction of the citadel of our faith, which has been blasted apart by our endless "holy" warring. This process in the household of God will be hastened if we follow the principles for all household renovations. We must forgive; we must clean house. We must ask for God to tip the small vessels in our hearts and spill the overflow of his love.

Probably in no other practice situation will we become so exercised in volunteering forgiveness as in the church. We are often insensitive to one another in this family, having no idea of the wounds we deliver, because we are inarticulate about those pains. Perhaps one day we will learn to be honest with each other, to gently sensitize one another, to say, "Whoops! That hurt. Forgive my touchiness but what you just said, what you just did brought me pain." (One day, we may also become so receptive to the whispers of the Holy Spirit, we will hear him speak to us about another's mute grief.) Until then, we must be ready to forgive without being asked.

Forgiveness should be preached from our pulpits. I am appalled by how often people say, "We really needed what you had to say. We've had little teaching on the subject." This preaching ought to come from men who have experienced its work. No one requires the release of this supernatural gift more than our battle-scarred ministers! Then church leaders must provide formats in which the works of forgiveness can be facilitated.

Granted, forgiveness is always a personal matter, but in the Body of Christ, it can often be stimulated on a corporate level. When we were pastoring, we provided our congregation with an opportunity to participate in specific prayers of forgiveness by handing them the following handout after a sermon on the topic. This sheet became a vehicle for life response. I am including portions here to aid churches who might be seeking to design a "Forgiveness Morning" of their own.

"Father, we bring to you all the relationships within our body, all the painful misunderstandings. It is our desire that we might be freed from all the pains that bind us. Hear our specific prayers for forgiveness."

I forgive people for all the things they haven't done—
—for no phone calls when I was absent or in great need of spirit.
—for the lack of a greeting, which seemed to be a deliberate cut.
—for not being invited into homes on hospitality nights, for not being included in evenings of fellowship.
—for no one caring for me as a person, but for everyone only wanting from me the things I can do for them or for this community.
—for those who have withheld love when I desperately needed love extended.
—for those who have insisted upon helping me in *their* way rather than in the way I needed help.

I forgive the things that have been said—
—the words, words, words, that harm me more than sticks and stones and sometimes damage me in deeper, more lasting ways.
—pious phrases telling me how to improve myself when I thought I was really making progress in that area.
—words traveling through third parties.
—criticism that tore the petals off some new flower God was nurturing in the hothouse of my soul.
—jealousy, sugar-coated in devious love, a truly bitter pill.
—those who so blithely report what other people feel, think, and say about me, especially the negative.
—gossip, pure and simple, aimed at me.

148

—people who have questioned my motives.

I forgive those in our body who have been inadequate friends—
—those who have rejected my tentative and feeble efforts to reach out.
—those who refuse to forgive me for things I have done that have damaged a relationship.
—those who don't know how to be a friend unless I do all the calling, seeking out, initiating.
—those who can never share beyond a superficial level, denying me invitation to their fellowship.
—those who know how to befriend me when I am in need, but cut off the relationship when I am functioning well.
—those who destroy a possible relationship because they "don't want to bother me," and consequently leave no foundation on which to build.

"We forgive, Father; be pleased to work the release of forgiveness in our hearts."

This liturgy of forgiveness can be adapted to the unique needs of specific congregations—in fact the person who adapts such a form for church business meetings may be overwhelmed with instant success and further marketing opportunities!

Another corporate aid might be to ask a congregation to respond to a message on forgiveness by writing, in their own words, specific prayers of forgiveness on a piece of paper. Then, invite all who wish to bring their papers to the front, fold them in the sight of all, and tear them in two. Perhaps when all have been discarded, there can be a burning ceremony to symbolize the way God obliterates the filthy rags of our despairing relationships.

After we have helped one another forgive, we will

149

have to undergo housecleaning. Corporate confession is an underranked, overlooked, powerful cathartic cleansing agent. I think a brawling body, struggling with the means of coming to love one another, hungering for the reality of God's Presence, desperately needs opportunities to tell one another of personal sin and beg for forgiveness.

By this I am not referring to a blow-by-blow description of all the lurid details. No, I am alluding to those sweet, brokenhearted statements of error we make when touched by God's convicting power. The opportunities for confession should be made available; they should not be manufactured.

The reason I am convinced of the necessity of voluntary public confession is that all major movements of revival throughout church history have documented the occurrence of this type of cathartic cleansing. The Book of Ezra records a sample: "While Ezra prayed and made confession, weeping and casting himself down before the house of God, a very great assembly . . . gathered to him out of Israel; for the people wept bitterly. . . . 'We have broken faith with our God and have married foreign women' " (10:1-3). Spiritual renewals, either private or corporate, are always characterized by a recognition of shortcoming. There is no classical spiritual renaissance recorded throughout time without accompanying confession.

I am comfortable with this recommendation for housecleaning because of strong scriptural precedent. James writes, "Is any one among you suffering? Let him pray. Is any cheerful? Let him sing praise. Is any among you sick? Let him call for the elders of the church, and let them pray over him, anointing him with oil in the name of the Lord; and the prayer of faith will save the sick man, and the Lord will raise him up; and if he has committed sins, he will be forgiven. Therefore confess your sins to one another, and pray for one another, that you may be healed. The prayer of a righteous man has great power in its effect"(5:13-16).

For years, I have interpreted these words to mean that the one in the hospital bed should confess his sins in order to receive healing. However, I have recently come to understand that the invalid *and the elders, as well as the congregation, must confess in order for God's great power to sweep through us,* renewing, restoring, reconciling, bringing spiritual renaissance to our lives.

Confess your sins one to another, and pray for one another, that you may be healed. What kind of healing is more important than a cure for the disease of lovelessness? Corporate confession is God's antidote against our chronic addiction to brawling.

We have forgiven; we have cleaned house. Now we tip our small pots of love which have been filled by God's affluence. We pray the prayer, "Lord, give me your love for this brother/sister within our body." God's love begins to fill us. He gives us glimpses of his viewpoint toward this person who annoys us. He grants us flashes of understanding. We start to love again.

We are now the parties responsible for initiating love. It is we who must start the doing, going, phoning, inviting, forgiving.

In is intriguing to me, a word person, that so many of the gifts of the Holy Spirit depend on the spoken word. The lists in 1 Corinthians 12 include: utterance of wisdom, utterance of knowledge, prophecy, various kinds of tongues, the interpretation of tongues. The Romans 12 listing contains prophecy, teaching, and exhortation. Of course, there are gifts that may or may not have anything to do with words, such as contributions, acts of mercy, or service rendered; but the majority deal with some sort of incarnated verbal expression.

Since all the gifts of the Holy Spirit are given for the purpose of ministry within the Body of Christ, I am convinced we have grossly underrated the creative, healing power of the right words. Emily Dickinson believed that words, greatly conceived and expressed, are sacramental in their efficacy. To state it another way, there is something of God in them. Peter writes, ". . . by the word of God heavens existed long ago. . . . But by the same word the heavens and earth that now exist have been stored up for fire . . ." (2 Pet. 3:5, 7). What power there is in godly words!

There is an interesting attitude conveyed by a short verse in Acts 12:24. "But the word of God grew and multiplied." The writer seems to look at that word as an entity unto itself. It is not the church that grew and multiplied—though that was happening. It was not the preaching of the word that was growing—but the word, the word unto itself. "The sword of the Spirit . . . is the word of God," reads Ephesians 6:17. Paul reminds his readers in 2 Timothy 1:9 that he is suffering and fettered like a criminal, "But the word of God is not fettered." We must allow this living thing to indwell us.

If only the Body of Christ, his Bride, would cease its declarations of war, its stockpiling of military armaments, its bloodying of the brethren. Perhaps our brawling could be ended if we realized how much feeding and nourishing and healing could be accomplished through the ministry of the verbal spiritual gifts. If we would concentrate on allowing the mind of Christ to so fill us that we would begin to speak his thoughts to one another, perhaps we could call a truce to our disputes. Maybe then, the Word that became flesh, "full of grace and truth," might be enfleshed within us. We need to experience this incarnation, one that is possible every moment and not limited to space or time—"the word of God abides in you" (1 John 2:14). Then the warring would certainly be terminated.

Part of the discipline of initiating love is the speaking to one another of God's words. Our tongues become his messengers, and we begin the work of recreation in another's broken, bruised soul. Our words become his tools, a surgeon's delicate equipment for cutting away scar tissue from past pains, clipping out threatening malignancies, but skilled enough to leave clean incisions that can heal. Our mouths breathe love to the loveless; they blow his breath to the suffocating.

The following few phrases I have collected from Proverbs may convince us of the possible sacramental efficacy of words: "Evil words destroy, godly skills rebuild. The words of the wise soothe and heal. The upright speak what is helpful. A soft answer turns away wrath. Gentle words cause life and health. Kind words are like honey, enjoyable and healthful. Ability to give wise advice satisfies like a good meal. Timely advice is as lovely as golden apples in a silver basket."

There can be something beyond the human in our initiating words of love. If we will allow it, God can be present in the things that we say. In order for this to occur, we are going to have to travel back to the place where we first started, to the household of the heart. "Out of the abundance of the heart, the mouth speaks," taught Christ. "The good man out of his good treasure brings forth good, and the evil man out of his evil treasure brings forth evil. I tell you, on the day of judgment men will render account for every careless word they utter; for by your words you will be justified, and by your words you will be condemned" (Matt. 12:34-37).

We have come full circle. If we are going to be vehicles of healing, bearing grace to the body, we must look into our own hearts. What passions rage within? What doors have been locked? What rooms have been violated with the storing of our secret filth? Forgiveness, cleansing, God's love—these are the ingredients that will enable us to be truly hospitable to one another in the church. We can learn to invite each other into our lives, to share the meals, the work, the joys and labors that are part and parcel of living together. We can love.

Once our hearts are inhabited by God, we will find it easier to extend the invitations. We will suddenly discover facility in sharing the innermost work of the Master Builder. We will move closer to that ideal, the family of God, the joint heirs in Christ, a place where there is no partiality, no favoritism, no discrimination; where we are no longer strangers and sojourners, where the gates are open wide. The words, "Why don't you come in?" will become familiar.

One day the Bride will walk that long aisle into eternity where she will meet her Bridegroom, King Jesus. Perhaps she will move in dignity, unblemished, limping no longer, shod in slippers of satin. Perhaps her hair will flow, silky from brushing, healthy and shining in the sun. Perhaps she will be adorned in white robes of righteousness, sacred vestments, costly garments. Perhaps, one day, she will be presented, beautiful and adored, unspotted in her innocence. She will be a fitting love for the Bridegroom whom some call Faithful and True.

I, for one, have great hopes.

LIFE RESPONSE

Find creative ways to play the "What's Good About Game." (Drop the "What's Bad About" part. There's enough of that in every church congregation!) In other words, discover the variety of means that exist to identify what is good in one another.

1. Write a note that expresses your positive feelings. Don't get bogged down in vague generalities—"You're really nice." Rather, discipline yourself to be specific—"I really appreciate your gentleness. Often I find that I am afraid of certain personalities, but I am never afraid of you."

2. In a small group of people who know each other, take turns telling each individual what his or her spiritual strengths are—"You have a real gift in teaching; without a doubt, you are a person who gives aid, who has mercy and shows it." It is not necessary that each person contribute for every individual, just that every one hears what is good about him.

3. Practice saying godly words on your own. Tell people what they mean to you. Encourage them; give them hope. Whisper "I love you" to the widow who hasn't heard those words for a while. State out loud, "That was a wonderful sermon" (or party or treasurer's report). State it a week after the sermon (or party or treasurer's report) has been given—then elaborate.

4. Upon being asked, say the words, "Of course, I forgive!"

I hope you enjoy the warm glow of love that always follows these exercises. It rarely fails; when we concentrate on the good, we call it out. Love draws love unto itself.

I have been here before,
  But when or how I cannot tell:
I know the grass beyond the door,
  The sweet keen smell,
The sighing sound, the lights around the shore:

You have been mine before—
  How long ago I may not know;
But just when at that swallow's soar
  Your neck turned so,
Some veil did fall—I knew it all of yore.

Has this been thus before?
  And shall not thus time's eddying flight
Still with our lives our love restore
  In death's despite?
And day and night yield one delight once more?

"SUDDEN LIGHT"
Dante Gabriel Rossetti

TWELVE
The Building Site: A Case Study

Casey and I were childhood friends. Her house was across the street from mine, and she was the oldest of nine children. Casey Kelly was her full name. One look and you knew her name had to be O'Hara or Riley or Shaughnessey. She was Irish to the core—red hair, freckles, and blue eyes. Without a doubt, she was my best friend.

We rarely fought. We held some deep discussions concerning our religions—I was Protestant and Casey was Catholic—but our disagreements never bordered on the fanatical. Surprisingly, we rarely got into trouble. There was too much work, I suppose, to allow much time for mischief. I was the eldest of three, and Casey was the head sibling of a long line of her parents' progeny. I can scarcely remember a cross word between us. We were immensely compatible.

Otherwise, we did all the things most girls do—we climbed trees, skinning our knees. We slept over. I was introduced to English muffins in the Kellys' kitchen one bright morning, and I've been hooked on them ever since. Dolls were out. Who needed them with all the real-life responsibilities? I think we assisted each other with various chores—these particular memories, however, are blissfully forgotten.

Ours was more of a summer friendship. Casey was a year older than I and thus was ahead of me in junior high as well as high school. It's not as though we were hostile. We just had differences during the academic year, a different circle of friends and activities. Once in a while we went ice skating, but mostly ours was a hot day, swimming pool, warm nights friendship.

Actually, Casey was extremely kind to associate with me at all. She was round and lovely, beautiful at all her ages, whereas I looked as though I might have been rescued from the last stages of labor camp confinement. I was a bean pole. Other of my friends' mothers would eye me skeptically and ask, "Karen, are you feeling all right?" I suppose they felt they should check me out in case I was the victim of some disease, some contagion I might pass on to their own robust offspring.

Mrs. Kelly, however, was considerate of me as one of the variety of kids running in and our of her house, and Casey, admirably, displayed most of her mother's graceful qualities. She even inherited the mellow, family singing voice, while I merely croaked, despite the fact that my father was a voice teacher.

We never dated one another's boyfriends. In fact, while in high school, Casey fell in love with one young man whom she eventually married. He was a Protestant from my own church, Grant Gustafson. (I wished his name had been O'Malley. Casey needed an Irish surname—but she was unconcerned, liking everything about him). One of the qualities she most admired was his brand of Christianity, and she soon became a Protestant, and a Baptist to boot.

After high school, we drifted our separate ways— Casey to setting up house and to having babies, and I to college and marriage and having babies of my own. Our paths rarely crossed except in the grocery store, and in time, we both moved out of town.

Imagine my delight, after David and I began pastoring in the middle of the city, when Casey and Grant showed up one Sunday morning. His company had transferred him back to the Midwest, and they had decided to try our congregation in their church-hopping odyssey. They loved it and became actively involved.

Casey and I picked up the loose ends of our friendship and began to relate, no longer as girls, but as women. Some things had changed—in fact, we had become completely different. Energetic, organized, a doer—my friend was now a perfect foil for me: exhausted, undisciplined, a thinker. We found that we got one another into perfectly awful messes. "Let's redecorate your downstairs," Casey said brightly to me one day. "Aren't you tired of never making any progress?"

I was. So we did. Tackling the easiest job first, we chiseled the plaster off a brick surface in the kitchen. (After several fruitless whacks, imagine my great relief at finding brick under the several inches of plaster facade!) Dust filtered onto every surface of my house, under every carefully closed door. We lugged cardboard boxes filled with tons of chunks of broken plaster out to the back alley.

The next job, an easier one, was to paper the ceiling in the kitchen. Amazingly, compared to doing the chimney, it was a fairly simple task. We walked casually across the catwalk made from boards and ladders, smoothly unrolling the pasted paper onto the ceiling above our heads. Sticking the fake styrofoam beams up was another matter, however. As usual, I had found a bargain. They had been on sale and only slightly warped, but they refused to adhere with the manufacturer's recommended adhesive.

Cleverly (desperately), we devised a system to provide the necessary tension to hold the beams in place until the glue adhered. Paint cans were stacked on chairs, which were piled on tables, with brooms and mop handles and curtain rods and measuring sticks of all lengths wedged between them and the recalcitrant blocks of foam stuck on the ceiling.

David came home that evening to find Casey and me filling in the gaps at opposite ends of our catwalk, our heads supplying the needed pressure. Looking all the world like two bedraggled statues, pillars in some forsaken temple, ravished by the elements and the ages, we couldn't have cared less about our appearances. The beams were finally sticking, the wallpaper looked marvelous, and we had held a wonderful conversation!

The simplest task we had saved for last. That was to steam off the old wallpaper, hidden under several coats of latex, in the dining room. Starting at eight o'clock one morning, we were still at it when two the next morning rolled around. We didn't finish until an hour later.

We had been forced to scrape each inch of wall. The hot water from our rented steam machine couldn't penetrate all that paint. Balancing on the scaffolding, one of us had to prop the tired elbow of the other holding the heavy, steaming appliance against the ceiling while the first one scraped with her free hand. The process was made all the more difficult because our labors had become extremely funny, and we were laughing. We hadn't worn makeup for two days, and the steam was dripping onto the remains of plaster dust, which had settled into our hair several projects before.

All of this retelling of tales simply goes to prove that Casey and I were good friends. Only a firm loyalty could have tolerated the extremes of our relationship. (And our childhood had been so normal, so promising!)

We had changed, however, in those growing years. Personality development progresses; it alters one. It was probably inevitable that our two strong wills would eventually clash. In time, a breach came in the gladsome, I-have-known-her-from-childhood relationship. To this day, I don't know what caused it. There were no harsh words; there was no date on the calendar marking an ugly incident. The wonderful/terrible projects we had shared, nevertheless, ceased. The intimacy fled. We barely talked at church. We gave one another grudging regard in small groups.

For most of my adult life, I have kept a prayer journal, but it was really only after the barriers went up between Casey and myself that I began to faithfully write in it. Consequently, I have the record of a case study in forgiveness.

I began to pray for a renewal in our relationship. For several years, I jotted this request down. Perhaps Casey had been slightly critical of me. I know that during this period in my life, the doors of my heart were slamming quickly on any who seemed negative toward our ministry. At any rate, I experienced my first taste of the supernatural release of forgiveness at a summer campgrounds by Lake Michigan.

Of course, upon coming home, I wanted all things

restored. I forgave my friend, which was rather difficult because I really had not understood what had thrown this curtain between us. After each prayer session regarding Casey, I would take myself in hand, make a phone call, extend an invitation, perform some sort of initiatory action. She was always lovely and responded to me warmly, but she never reached out to me (at least, I couldn't see her reaching out), and the closeness never returned. Then the curtain would fall again.

"I refuse to call." I would temper tantrum before the Lord, time and again. "It's always me who does the reaching. Casey doesn't want our old friendship. She doesn't care about it. She has new relationships. I'm tired of always having to be the one who makes the effort."

Often, during this period, I had to drive several hours alone to some destination where I had been invited to speak. Frequently, I would invite a member of the church to accompany me, and we would use the time to become better acquainted. On one of these occasions, I took my reluctant courage in hand and approached Casey to see if she would like to come. To my great surprise, she accepted.

While traveling for several hours there, and then several hours back, our relationship was renewed. We were suddenly friends again. After years of awkwardness, things were almost the same as they had been when I was a skinny preteen and Casey was the beauty of the block. We never once referred to the wall that had been between us. We did not dissect what had gone wrong. It didn't matter.

One other notation in my notebook records a last temper tantrum in regard to my relationship with Casey. It was written after our restoration. I was complaining to God because that Sunday morning after a sermon on forgiveness, I heard him telling me that I should write a note to my friend and ask her to forgive me for causing the breach in the friendship!

I stamped my feet all over the household of my soul! I pounded on the walls! Ask Casey to forgive me? Why, I was the one who had wanted things to return to normal. I was the one who had worked at the relationship (of course, there was that surprise birthday party she had planned for me)—but I was the one who had done most of the reaching!

I wrote the note.

Dear Casey,

After this morning's service, I feel impressed by the Holy Spirit to ask you to forgive me for anything I might have done that caused a breach in our relationship. I love you and want our friendship to grow.

Please accept this apology and consider it an indication of my permission to inform me of anything I might do in the future that would endanger our closeness.

Much love,
Karen

The note was received, I'm sure, but nothing was said about it, and no return letter came winging my way. The lovely truth of it is, however, that there was no need for more words. Forgiveness releases us from keeping count, from the insistence to even scores.

Since that time, the two of us have been contractors working together on the joint building site of our souls. We are restructuring a living relationship, planning a new commons, a meeting place of our adult spirits. Oh, we still get each other into all sorts of messes. Recently, we thought we had permission to dig up an alley in the city that was scheduled to be destroyed due to planned construction. (I was the one who needed the paving bricks for a new patio.)

Each brick weighed eight pounds, and after we had transported several heavy, station-wagon loads over the whizzing expressways, we decided to rent a truck with a hydraulic lift. While swinging the unwieldy pick to loosen the pavement, and wiping the soot of years from our eyes and faces, we looked up to see five Chicago squad cars (count them—one, two, three, four, five!) screech to a halt beside us, their red lights blazing.

"Put dem bricks back in d'alley, lady," the police captain ordered, none too politely, I complied, and we drove the truck back to the rental yard—empty.

This has to be the proof of friendship, a loyalty so enduring it will face the threat of possible arrest, the vision of cooling off in Cook County Jail. Yet there is more to our relationship. There is a regular sharing of who we are, a weekly session in which we talk about the important areas of our lives, when we hold one another accountable to spiritual growth, when we listen to delights and fears, when we give to one another the gifts of love.

We have invited each other into our lives. How lovely to be included in this invitation.

What? You want me? I'm a nobody, an insignificant person standing here on the sidelines of life. You want me to come into that great house standing in the middle of town? You want to show me the vestibules festooned with garlands, the new turrets spiraling upward that house the happy playrooms of your children? You want my opinion on which tapestries to hang on the imported stone walls of the dining hall?

You want me? You want me to walk the garden paths

with you and enjoy the roses, sniff the fragrance of rosemary, thyme, and lemon verbena? You want to tell me about the rambling lawns and spreading verandas? You want to point me in the direction of the Master Builder who is at work in your soul?

I'd love to come in. I've been waiting so long to be included in the invitation to the open house in your soul. I've wanted to pick up some ideas for my own remodeling projects. I've longed to sit by your side before the fire and tell tales and weave laughter. I'd like to whisper legends about the Master Builder myself. Thank you for inviting me.

Forgiveness? I know it works. I have experienced the supernatural results of it. I have concluded that it is worth practicing again and again, without being asked. I know the surprising warmth of God's love filling me when before I have felt only coldness. The pot has tipped in my soul, spilling into the life of another. I have learned to ask, "Forgive me, please." I have been willing to bear the pain.

Forgiveness works. Ask Casey!

LIFE RESPONSE

There is an intriguing verse in Ezekiel 37: 9. "Prophesy to the breath, prophesy, son of man, and say to the breath, Thus says the Lord God: Come from the four winds, O breath, and breathe upon these slain, that they may live."

I love to think about these phrases when I am laboring over dull words, empty sentences. My prayer is that he will breathe himself into my work, that he will fill these dead nouns and verbs with new life.

God is also the One who can breathe new life into slain

relationships. He can fill the valley of our dry bones with re-creation. Perhaps you have a friendship that needs resurrection. Invite the Spirit to come and begin his breathing in you. Then wait and discover what vitality can be restored in that once-dead companionship.

"Breathe, O breath, upon these slain, that they may live."

A Bible Study on Forgiveness

to accompany *Key to an Open Heart*
by Wayne Nelson

An Introduction

Here are fourteen Bible studies which will help you gain further Biblical perspective on the subject of forgiveness. These studies are designed to be used as discussion starters for small groups or for your own individual reading and meditation. Be sure to read the book first, then work through these studies, integrating the Biblical studies here with the observations and help offered in *Key to an Open Heart* by Karen Mains.

Nothing is as devastating or destructive to the human spirit as guilt. The consciousness of our sin, our imperfection, our separation from an awesome, majestic and infinitely holy God can crush us as completely as a heavy millstone pulverizes a grain of wheat. But to all those who find themselves under this terrible burden, the Scriptures proclaim that the God who is perfect in holiness is also powerful to save. No matter how strong or how real the guilt of our sin, it is no match for the forgiveness freely offered us through the Lord Jesus Christ and His sacrifice.

These studies will help you focus on some of the great Bible texts on forgiveness. As you meditate on these passages and work through the questions, we hope you gain a better grasp the message of Scripture. The promise is that by faith, the grip of guilt on our lives will be loosened and ultimately destroyed.

But the Bible, in speaking of forgiveness, warns us against imagining that we can receive God's pardoning grace without extending that grace to others. After all,

169

it was Christ Himself who taught us to pray: "And forgive us our debts, as we forgive our debtors." Thus the studies seek to balance those passages which speak of God's forgiveness toward us with those that speak of our forgiveness to others.

Study One
Forgiveness After the Fall

Life Need:
Do you remember your Junior High days? Something is lost, but the searching party doesn't admit any blame. Instead, "somebody has stolen it." Many people go through life blaming other people for their own shortcomings, and most of us do it sometimes. This study looks at Adam, Eve, and God's forgiveness.

Bible Learning:
Genesis 1:26-4:2

Bible Application:
1. What did the first couple lose or forfeit as a result of their disobedience?

2. What was God's purpose in seeking out and questioning Adam and Eve?

3. What were Adam and Eve's motives in responding to God?

4. What was required for Adam and Eve to experience God's forgiveness?

5. What did the birth of Cain and Abel indicate about the blessing God had originally pronounced on Adam and Eve?

6. Could human history have continued without God's forgiveness? Why or why not?

7. Would you agree with the statement that "Forgiveness is priceless"?

8. Does the quality of one's confession affect the quality of God's forgiveness?

Summary Thought:
Only God's forgiveness can restore to sinful man the possibility of experiencing His blessings.

Life Application:
In your relation to God and others, do your admissions of wrong-doing involve accepting responsibility or rather shifting the blame? In your opinion, what would be the elements of a legitimate and acceptable confession?

Study Two
The Faith to Forgive

Life Need:
Have you ever experienced deep hurt from a family member or someone very close to you? Most of us have; sometimes the person causing the hurting is doing so out of deliberate malice, but more often the hurt comes out of neglect or even good motives. Does it

seem that it is more difficult to forgive someone who is close to you than someone you hardly know?

Bible Learning:
Genesis 37, 39-40, 42-45, 50

Bible Application:
1. Was the precise physical relationship between Joseph and his brothers the same as that between Cain and Abel (Genesis 4) and Jacob and Esau (Genesis 25)?

2. Why did Joseph's brothers develop a hatred toward him?

3. What consideration(s) induced Joseph's brothers to sell him as a slave rather than kill him?

4. Who else, besides his brothers, wronged Joseph intentionally or unintentionally?

5. Is there evidence that Joseph had already forgiven his brothers even before he saw them?

6. What enabled Joseph to forgive them?

7. Was it easy for Joseph's brothers to "feel" forgiven?

8. Could it be said that Joseph is a type of Christ?

Summary Thought:
The power to forgive comes from the faith that God can use our suffering for the good of others.

Life Application:

Can you identify a specific circumstance in your life in which others caused you to suffer? When it occurred, did you have the spiritual resources to respond as Joseph did? What if you experienced an injustice today?

Study Three
Forgiveness and the Fear of the Lord

Life Need:

Some of the great pieces of drama have been on the theme of revenge. The desire to strike back at those who hurt you is a core value to the human condition. Yet, doing good to those who hate you is central to Christian teaching. How do you reacted when someone has done something bad to you? What were the results later?

Bible Learning:

I Samuel 24, 26

Bible Application:

1. Did David permit circumstances to dictate his course of action?

2. What convictions prevented David from taking Saul's life the first time such an opportunity presented itself (chapter 24)? the second time (chapter 26)?

3. Does a forgiving spirit mean one should not confront a wrongdoer?

4. Does forgiving others require us to trust them?

5. The second time David spared Saul's life did he evidence a greater or lesser degree of sensitivity toward the person of the king?

6. Does our responsibility to forgive others depend on their repentance?

7. Does our forgiveness of others free them from the obligation to seek God's forgiveness?

Summary Thought:
Whether we forgive others depends not on what we think about what they have done to us but rather on what we think about God.

Life Application:
In life today, what are the means at our disposal for getting back at a person who has wronged us? In the light of David's actions here and his subsequent experience, why is it a wiser and safer course of action to forgive others rather than to avenge ourselves?

Study Four
Confession through Cross-examination

Life Need:
As you have watched your children or those of others, have you noticed how some children will be very tender toward doing what is right and will confess quickly a wrong-doing? Others need to be "dragged,

kicking and screaming" toward the point of confession. How difficult is it for you to confess to God your short-comings? How difficult is it to confess to someone else?

Bible Learning:
   2 Samuel 11-12

Bible Application:
1. Once David had committed adultery and learned that he might be found out, what did he do?

2. How long did David spend in an unrepentant condition?

3. What means did the prophet use to bring David to his knees? Why did the story he told have such a powerful impact on David?

4. What indications are there that David sincerely repented of his sin?

5. Did God's forgiveness mean that David was to get off scot-free?

6. Why is the proverbial saying "Be sure your sin will find you out" true?

Summary Thought:
   Our assurance of God's forgiveness can only begin when we are brought to our knees.

Life Application:
   No matter what our spiritual experience or previ-

ous performance, the sin of David stands as a perpetual warning and reminder that we can never consider ourselves immune from temptation. We can only be sure that, when we sin, the Lord is concerned to use whatever is necessary to bring us back to Him, no matter how painful or difficult for us it is. Do your confessions of sin tend to be spontaneous or forced?

Study Five
From Pain to Praise

Life Need:
Do you remember what you felt like after confessing and asking forgiveness? Was it with a continuing feeling of dread, or did you experience a sense of relief and renewal? How did you feel about God during those times?

Bible Learning:
Psalm 32 and 51

Bible Application:
1. In confessing his sin, on what basis could David hope to approach God?

2. What did David's sin cause him to realize about himself?

3. Besides God's forgiveness, for what else does David ask?

4. What does David promise God as a sign of his seriousness? (Psalm 32):

5. What is the blessing David celebrates at the beginning of this psalm?

6. What led David to confess his sin?

7. What should be the response of the believer to God's forgiveness?

Summary Thought:
God's forgiveness transforms our suffering for sin into a celebration of His grace.

Life Application:
As Christians, we praise God for His blessings and grace in our lives, but when was the last time we expressed to Him publicly our gratitude for His forgiveness of our sins? Why is it easier to thank the Lord for such things as physical well-being and material benefits than for His forgiveness? And why is it important to emphasize our thankfulness for God's pardon of our sin?

Study Six
The Pouting Prophet of Pardon

Life Need:
Are there people with whom you've come in contact or you've seen in the media who you would have difficulty sitting next to in church? What are your feelings toward these people. What if you knew that God wanted you to reach out and invite them to your home for Christian hospitality? Could you do it?

Bible Learning:
The Book of Jonah

Bible Application:
1. Why does God instruct Jonah to go to Nineveh?

2. How do we know that it was not a fear of confessing his faith before the heathen that kept Jonah from going to Nineveh?

3. Can we say that when Jonah did finally obey God his obedience was from the heart?

4. What was (were) God's purpose(s) in commanding Jonah to proclaim His judgment against Nineveh?

5. How do we know the Ninevites truly repented?

6. What about God's character did Jonah resent?

7. Explain in your own words the point God attempts to make with Jonah at the end of the book.

Summary Thought:
As God's people we are responsible to call men to repentance, not to decide who is worthy of divine forgiveness.

Life Application:
Our hesitancy to witness sometimes comes from a fear of being misunderstood or ridiculed. But is it possible that at times we are silent because we don't believe some people are worthy to hear the gospel message? It is reported that someone once asked a great

theologian what he would have said to Adolph Hitler, if they had ever met. The man replied: "I would have told him 'Jesus died for your sins'." Would our response have been the same as his?

Study Seven
Experiencing a Full and Final Forgiveness

Life Need:
Many people will say about a good situation, "It's too good to be true." When finally convinced it is true, they will mutter, "It's too good to last." Have you ever felt that way about being forgiven by God? By others?

Bible Learning:
Jeremiah 31:31-34

Bible Application:
1. What does the term "covenant" suggest about the character of the new relationship between the Lord and His people?

2. Who is the principle subject of the actions described in this passage?

3. In what ways does this new covenant differ from the old covenant God made with Israel in the days of Moses?

4. To what exactly is God referring when He speaks of putting His "law" into the hearts and minds of His people?

5. What kind of knowledge of God is implied when God says: "They will all know me . . . " (v. 34)?

6. Upon what, in your opinion, is the forgiveness of which God speaks (v. 34) based?

7. When would this new covenant be inaugurated, according to this passage?

Summary Thought:
Real forgiveness of sin comes to us only as we are drawn by the Lord into a personal relationship with Him.

Life Application:
So often, when we pray, we ask God either to forgive our sins or to keep us from sin. While such prayer is consistent with that which Christ taught us, the Bible speaks of the answer to sin as involving a deeper and more intimate knowledge of God which comes through our personal relationship with Him. If you were to characterize your knowledge of God according to one of the following terms, which one would best describe it and why? One of whom I have heard; someone I know by name; a casual acquaintance; a friend; a close friend; my best friend; my father.

Study Eight
The Foundation of Forgiveness

Life Need:
How difficult is it to accept something for nothing?

Some people can do it quite easily. Others are fiercely independent and believe that nothing which is worth something can be given without payment of some kind. This second group tends to have a much more difficult time of accepting God's "free gifts." They feel they somehow must "earn" it through their actions. Have you tried to "pay back" people for what they have done for yhou? Can you accept gifts from others without being compulsive about "paying it back?"

Bible Learning:
Isaiah 52:13-53:12

Bible Application:
1. Of whom is the person this passage describes the servant?

2. Does the prophet suggest that the servant's appearance is in any way remarkable?

3. Does Isaiah speak of us and of the servant as "sheep" in the same way?

4. How many times in this passage is it said that the servant suffered for the sins of others and how many times does it say that his suffering was for his own sins?

5. What in the passage indicates that the servant's suffering and death was a sacrifice for sin?

6. Is there anything in this passage that suggests the suffering and death of the servant is the final sacrifice for sin?

Summary Thought:
Our sins can be forgiven simply and solely because Jesus died for them.

Life Application:
In our relations with other people, we find ourselves from time to time having to make amends for mistakes we have made or hurts we have caused. Unfortunately, in our relationship with God, we can sometimes consciously or unconsciously attempt to "make up" for our sins. Can you think of a time you have in some way tried to do this? Why is this wrong, according to this passage?

Study Nine
The Miracle of Forgiveness

Life Need:
Some people find it fairly easy to forgive most acts against them. Others find it extremely difficult to forgive even the smallest slight or hurt. Most of us would have difficulty forgiving someone who has threatened our lives or the lives of someone we love. So what about the saying, "To err is human; to forgive, divine?"

Bible Learning:
Matthew 9:1-8

Bible Application:
1. When Jesus pronounced the paralytic man's sins forgiven, to what does the text say He was responding?

2. Why do you think some of those present there assumed that in doing this Jesus had committed the sin of blasphemy?

3. How did Jesus' healing of the paralytic respond to the charge of blasphemy that some there had made (if only in their minds) against Him?

4. Do you think Jesus healed the paralytic only to demonstrate His authority to those who were questioning Him?

5. For what specifically did those who witnessed these events praise God?

6. Do you think that Jesus' authority to forgive sin needs continuing miraculous confirmation in our day? Why or why not?

Summary Thought:
   Jesus' divine authority to forgive was demonstrated by His divine power to heal.

Life Application:
   Our tendency is perhaps the opposite of that of the Jews of Jesus' day. We can tend to take forgiveness for granted while marveling at miracles. But for the Jews, it seems, the fact that Jesus could pronounce sins forgiven was even more remarkable (or unbelievable) than that. If someone were to ask you if you had ever experienced a miracle, do you think your forgiveness by God would qualify? Why or why not?

Study Ten
The Fruit of Forgiveness (Part 1)

Life Need:

No matter how willingly we do something, we almost all desire to be thanked for an act of kindness or good will. And the same holds true for the act of forgiveness. Obviously, since forgiving is a two-way street, we also need to look at thankfulness for forgiveness road that goes in both directions.

Bible Learning:

Luke 7:36-50

Bible Application:

1. Why do you think someone invited Jesus to dinner in his home?

2. In your opinion, did the visit with Jesus go as Simon had thought or planned? Why or why not?

3. How many differences were there between Simon and the woman?

4. What conclusion did Simon draw on the basis of the contact between the woman and Jesus, and why?

5. What conclusion did Jesus draw on the basis of the differences between Simon's treatment of Him and that of the woman?

6. Is Jesus teaching that forgiveness results from love or love from forgiveness? How can you be sure?

Summary Thought:
Our understanding of God's forgiveness is best measured by our gratitude for His forgiveness.

Life Application:
Since Christ is not physically present now as He was then, is it possible for us to imitate what this woman did? Try to think of a way to tangibly express to God your gratitude for His forgiving grace in your life. Can you think of something that would not necessarily involve an explicitly religious setting or act (such as putting more money in the offering plate on Sunday)?

Study Eleven
The Fruit of Forgiveness (Part 2)

Life Need:
While we sometimes recite the golden rule, "Do unto others as we would have them do unto us," we are also tempted to keep track of the score, just to make sure the instances of doing don't dramatically outweigh the instances of receiving. But is that what Christ really teaches?

Bible Learning:
Matthew 18:21-35

Bible Application:
1. What prompted the parable that Jesus told here?

2. In the parable, what was the King's response when the debtor begged for an opportunity to repay what he owed?

3. What happened when the debtor left the king's presence and encountered someone who owed him money?

4. How did the two debts compare in size? (Hint: One talent ranged in value from $250 to $1600, according to the metal involved, while a denarius was worth about 18 cents.)

5. Can you think of how the first debtor in the parable might have rationalized his action toward the second?

6. How does Jesus interpret and apply the parable?

7. In your opinion, what does the expression "forgive from the heart" mean?

Summary Thought:
Our forgiveness by God obligates us to forgive others.

Life Application:
Is it legitimate for God to require us to forgive others if we are to enjoy His forgiveness? To put this question in perspective, why not keep track of the number of times you sense the need to ask God's forgiveness in a period of one week? Then compare this with the number of times you think others should ask forgiveness of you in the same period of time? How do the two figures compare?

Study Twelve
"Father, Forgive Them!"

Life Need:
When you read the papers, do you often think, "What if that horrible crime had been done to my family?" Or maybe you don't need to even imagine someone really hurting you, either physically or psychologically. In any case, we must understand the forgiveness process so that we can forgive as we have been forgiven.

Bible Learning:
Luke 23:26-49; Acts 6:1-7:60

Bible Application:
1. Who were those who demonstrated a commitment to Jesus to the very end?

2. In what ways does our Lord evidence a selfless attitude in the midst of His sufferings?

3. What is the significance of Jesus's prayer recorded in verse 34?

4. Of what was Stephen accused by some of his fellow Jews?

5. How does Stephen say the Jews treated their God-given leaders such as Joseph, Moses and the prophets?

6. According to Stephen, what was the greatest crime of the Jews?

7. How does Stephen demonstrate the extent of his Christ-like spirit?

Summary Thought:
The expression of a forgiving spirit is an intercessory ministry.

Life Application:
What has been the greatest wrong that has ever been committed against you? What significance should the example and actions of the Lord Jesus and Stephen have for us when we are the victims of injustice? How should we pray for our persecutors?

Study Thirteen
Facilitating Forgiveness

Life Need:
Remember when two of your friends were at odds with each other? You wondered if you could do something to help heal the wound between the two people, that would bring these two people back into a good relationship with each other. There is something special in the mediation of a trusted third party. Here's how Paul provided that service for two of his friends.

Bible Learning:
Philemon

Bible Application:
1. On whose behalf does Paul write to Philemon?

2. For what does Paul recommend Philemon?

3. What had been the previous relationship between Philemon and Onesimus?

4. What was the new relationship that now existed between them, according to Paul?

5. On what basis does Paul appeal to Philemon to forgive Onesimus?

6. What leverage does Paul use in encouraging Philemon to do what he asks of him?

Summary Thought:
Facilitating forgiveness between fellow Christians is our spiritual responsibility.

Life Application:
There are times when our responsibility is neither to forgive nor be forgiven, but rather to encourage reconciliation between others. Do you personally know of Christians who need to forgive one another? What action could you take to effect their reconciliation?

Study Fourteen
Foundation for Fellowship

Life Need:
"They shall know you are Christians by your love." That wonderful insight is often applied to an outreach love. Yet, the nonChristian world sits back and watches with amusement the infighting between Christian leaders or between major groups of Christians. The others miss the fact that the love of God is the glue that

should provide a fellowship among believers, and the pot for the glue of fellowship is forgiveness. How important a part does forgiveness play in helping grow your love for others?

Bible Learning:
1 John 1-2

Bible Application:
1. To what kinds of fellowship does John refer in the opening verses of chapter one?

2. How would you define the term "fellowship"?

3. What attitudes or actions make fellowship with God impossible?

4. What attitudes or actions are essential if we are to enjoy God's fellowship?

5. From what John says, is it possible to separate our fellowship with God from our fellowship with other Christians?

6. Besides forgiveness, what does God do for us in response to our confession?

7. How do we know that the blood of Christ is sufficient to cleanse us from all our sins?

Summary Thought:
God's full and complete forgiveness in Christ is the necessary foundation of our fellowship with Him and with other Christians.

Life Application:
We know that unconfessed sin makes fellowship with God impossible. But have we ever realized that when we are "out of fellowship" with God we are also "out of fellowship" with our fellow believers? Have you been guilty of compartmentalizing your relationship with God and that with other Christians?